kitchen
revelry

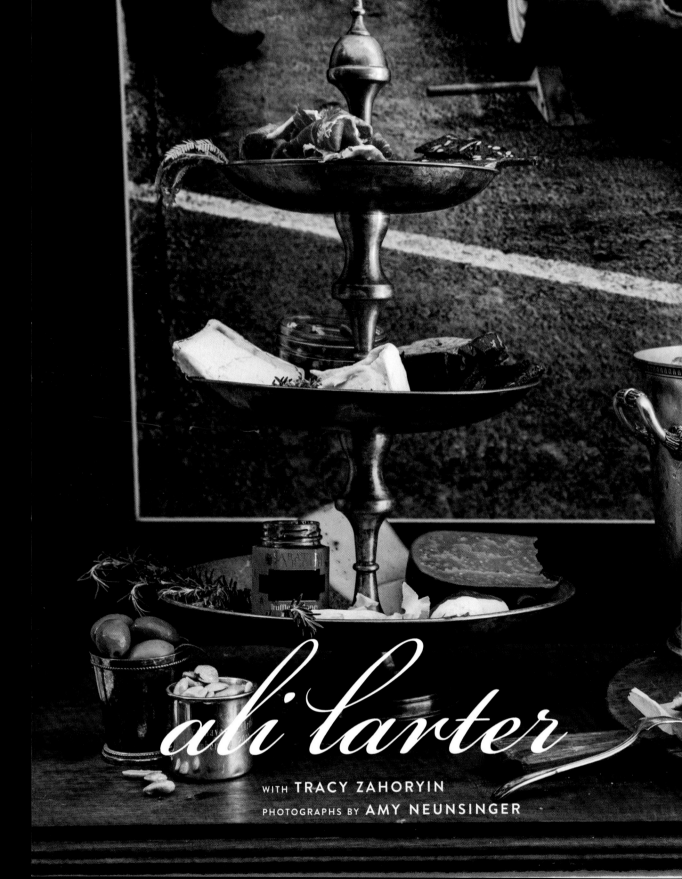

ali larter

WITH TRACY ZAHORYIN

PHOTOGRAPHS BY AMY NEUNSINGER

kitchen
revelry

a year of festive menus from my home to yours

ST. MARTIN'S PRESS
NEW YORK

www.stmartins.com

Book design by Laura Klynstra

Library of Congress Cataloging-in-Publication Data available upon request.

ISBN 978-1-250-03635-3 (hardcover)
ISBN 978-1-250-03883-8 (e-book)

St. Martin's Press books may be purchased for educational, business, or promotional use. For information on bulk purchases, please contact Macmillan Corporate and Premium Sales Department at 1-800-221-7945, extension 5442, or write specialmarkets@macmillan.com.

First Edition: September 2013

10 9 8 7 6 5 4 3 2 1

To Hayes and Theodore,
illumination,
you make my heart soar.

What is a Reveler?

A reveler is someone who loves sharing their passion for good times. A reveler is resourceful—overcoming obstacles with some sweat and a splash of sass. A reveler knows true lasting experiences are thoughtful, not expensive. A reveler is all about fabulous fresh foods, an adventurous spirit, and effortless style—one part Zen master, one part MacGyver, and two parts Rita Hayworth.

Contents

INTRODUCTION 1

4

september

Cooking School 7

Savoring the Last Bites
of Summer 23

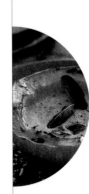

30

october

Harvest Party 33

Full Moon Party 43

94

january

Detox 97

Wanderlust Supper 107

116

february

Sweethearts Soirée 119

Super Bowl Party 125

170

may

Earth Mother's Brunch 173

Bar Was a Bust 187

194

june

Wine Tasting Evening 197

El Diablo 207

50

november

Out-of-Town Guests 53

Friends Thanksgiving 59

70

december

Tree-Trimming Cocktail Party 73

New Year's Eve Dinner 85

132

march

Movie Night Meals 135

Slumber Party 145

154

april

Alfresco Lunch 157

Spring Clothing Swap 165

210

july

Americana BBQ 219

Dinner at Dusk 229

236

august

Midsummer Night's Dream 239

Tuesday Night, No Reason 253

ACKNOWLEDGMENTS 256 INDEX 259

strada di ogni città c
sogna di diventare "qualcuno"
cato che deve disperatament

Introduction

This book was inspired by a disaster: My first dinner party! I was a young, struggling actress living in a fourth-floor walk-up above Pete's Tavern in New York City. I was trying to make new friends and had invited a few people over for dinner. In an attempt to make it a perfect evening, I planned an overly ambitious and complicated menu and soon realized I was in way over my head. My guests waited . . . and waited; I could *feel* them getting hungrier by the minute. Stressed, I took refuge in libations. And it was only downhill from there: my air-conditioning broke, I burnt my hand trying to light a flambé, and just to add to the drama, a mouse ran across my living room! I was tipsy, burned, and totally embarrassed. After my guests left, having barely picked at their dinner, I called my mom and burst into tears, swearing never to host another dinner party again.

Well, I have gotten past that disastrous evening. In fact, I learned a lot from it. Whether acting in a movie or following a recipe I was consumed with "getting it right" and "not messing up." I had always put a lot of pressure on myself. That night taught me to focus more on enjoying the process and to find beauty in imperfection. Nowadays I don't shy away from doing something because I'm worried I'll fail or a dish won't come out right. I know now that had I let that disastrous evening stop me I would have missed out on so much! That's what *Kitchen Revelry* is about: the process, not the outcome. So much happens around the dining room table: laughter, sharing, and even a little debauchery. So let this book inspire you to cook, invite friends over, and enjoy delicious food. Savor life.

My love of cooking started at a young age, growing up with fun-filled dinners with my family in Cherry Hill, New Jersey, where my mom made the kitchen the sanctuary of the house. As I grew older and my work took me to places from Italy to India, my horizons were broadened. All these places made culinary impressions, whether it was walking through Italian open-air markets, sitting in the kitchen of a Mumbai home, or talking to a baker on Spring Street.

The recipes in this book reflect these cherished moments, memories, and tastes. They reflect how I choose to celebrate the spirit of every occasion throughout the year. I photographed this book in my home with all my friends and family. Each occasion is built around a complete menu. Through laughter and tears, I've experimented, carefully tested, and assembled them with my friend and partner on this book, Tracy Zahoryin. We've eliminated the guesswork for you. These menus include my go-to recipes that you can whip up in an instant, my "best of the best" when you want to pull out all the stops, and my favorite entertaining ideas that are simple, chic and sexy.

Kitchen Revelry is a table full of luscious foods . . . friends old and new. It's about looking up to see lipstick-smudged glasses, a sink full of dirty dishes, pools of wax dripping from burning candles, and creating the memories of a great time. Move forward fearlessly, trust your taste, and pop the next bottle of champagne!

Ali Larter
xx

september

Cooking school

September is back-to-school month, and since a reveler is a kid at heart and always willing to learn, this month we are going to cooking school. My cooking school is all my go-to recipes I've been making for years, ones I pull out of my back pocket whether I want to enjoy the food alone or dazzle a crowd.

PARTY OF 2 TO 4

Vodka Martini with Cerignola Olives 8

Classic French Omelette 9

Shallot Vinaigrette with Simple Salad 9

Charcuterie 101 10

Roasted Chicken 12

Turkey Braciola 13

New York Steak with Herb Butter 16

Ricotta Meatballs with Chianti Sauce 19

Cauliflower-Reggiano Puree 20

German Chocolate Cupcakes 21

Vodka martini with cerignola olives

SERVES 2

Everyone should know how to make a perfect martini. So Bond. In goes the olive, out go your troubles.

Ice cubes

½ ounce dry vermouth (1 tablespoon)

6 ounces premium vodka
   (¾ cup)

2 Cerignola olives

Fill a cocktail shaker with ice. Add the vermouth and shake vigorously to coat the ice; pour out any remaining liquid. Add the vodka to the shaker and shake vigorously. Strain into two chilled martini glasses equally; add an olive to each glass and serve.

Classic french omelette

SERVES 1

This classic French omelette—inspired by my travels and a Youtube video by Julia Child—is good morning or night. I like mine with raclette, a semi-firm swiss cheese that melts beautifully, and simple greens tossed with shallot vinaigrette.

3 large eggs

1 tablespoon unsalted butter

2 ½ tablespoons grated raclette cheese

Sea salt and freshly ground black pepper, to taste

1 teaspoon chopped fresh parsley

In a bowl, whisk the eggs. Melt the butter in a medium nonstick skillet over medium-high heat until hot. Pour the eggs into the skillet. Swirl the skillet for 1 minute and continuously move a silicone spatula through the eggs in a figure eight. While the center of the eggs are still moist, remove the skillet from the heat and sprinkle the cheese over the eggs. Return the skillet to the heat, fold two sides of the eggs over the cheese. Flip omelette onto plate and sprinkle with salt and pepper. Garnish with chopped parsley and serve.

Shallot vinaigrette with simple salad

MAKES APPROXIMATELY ½ CUP VINAIGRETTE

This is an everyday dressing that is wonderful on all variations of lettuces and vegetables. It's a welcome change from bottled dressing and so easy to make.

5 tablespoons extra-virgin olive oil

1 tablespoon minced shallot

1 tablespoon red wine vinegar

2 teaspoons fresh lemon juice

½ teaspoon agave syrup

½ teaspoon Dijon mustard

¼ teaspoon sea salt

¼ teaspoon freshly ground black pepper

6 ounces mixed lettuces

Combine all the ingredients in a small bowl. Whisk vigorously until emulsified. Toss the vinaigrette with the lettuce and serve.

Charcuterie 101

I could live my life on a charcuterie plate, there's always some variation of one being served at my house. The cheese, a soft, a hard, a goat, a bleu; champagne grapes and blackberries; and prosciutto and salami all packed together on a wood board. Buy whatever you love or let these ideas inspire you. Quality cheeses and meats are key. Aesthetically, the canvas should have an artfully messy look, clustered, and overflowing with abundance. Fill it in with seasonal fruits or chutneys, crackers, and torn up baguettes. Remember to crumble some of your cheese so that it looks inviting, and stab in a few small knives for additional cutting.

A classic charcuterie is only meats, but I like to pack mine with everything. For larger parties, plan for about 2 ounces each, meat and cheese, per person. Always serve your charcuterie selections at room temperature for the most flavor. My favorite bite is raisin bread with a chunk of aged gouda and a drizzle of truffle honey.

MEATS
Prosciutto
Mortadella
Fennel Salami
Soppressata
Serrano Ham

CHEESE
Triple-Crème Brie
Humbolt Fog
Truffle Cheese
La Tur
Manchego

Aged Sharp Cheddar
Aged Gouda
Chevre with Herbs
Roquefort
Stilton

FRUITS
Champagne Grapes
Figs
Blackberries

FINISHING TOUCHES
Artichoke Hearts
Cornichons

Olives
Caper berries
Marcona Almonds
Truffle Honey
Fig Chutneys
Quince paste

BREADS AND CRACKERS
Crusty French Bread
Raisin Walnut Bread
Water Crackers
Artisanal Crackers
Crisps

Roasted chicken

SERVES 4

This recipe takes your basic roasted chicken to the next level. I promise you this is the juiciest bird you can make! Make it a one-pot dinner by adding potatoes, carrots, or any root vegetables you want. Always let your chicken rest for at least 10 minutes, tented with foil, to keep it succulent.

One 3- to 4-pound whole organic chicken, rinsed inside and out, patted dry

4 tablespoons Herb Butter, softened, divided (see recipe, page 16)

1 lemon, cut in half

3 fresh rosemary sprigs

Kosher salt and freshly ground black pepper, to taste

2 tablespoons extra-virgin olive oil

Preheat the oven to 450°F. Starting at the neck end of the chicken, carefully slide your hand between the skin and breast meat to loosen the skin. Using your fingertips, gently rub 2 tablespoons of the herb butter over the breast meat under the skin. Place the lemon halves, 2 rosemary sprigs, and the remaining 2 tablespoons herb butter in the main cavity of the chicken. Close the cavity with the remaining rosemary sprig, threading it through both sides of the cavity opening. Generously season the chicken with salt and pepper.

Heat the oil in a heavy, large ovenproof skillet (preferably cast-iron) over medium-high heat. Place the chicken, breast side down, in the skillet and sear for 2 minutes. Using tongs, turn the chicken over and sear on the second side for 2 minutes. Place the skillet with the chicken in the oven and roast, basting halfway through cooking, until the juices run clear when the thigh is pierced with a fork, and an instant-read thermometer inserted into the thickest part of the thigh registers 160°F, 45 to 60 minutes total. Remove the chicken from the oven. Tent the chicken with foil and let rest for 10 minutes.

Cut the chicken into serving pieces and place on plates. Spoon the juices over the chicken and serve. (See pages 4–5 for photo.)

Turkey braciola

SERVES 8

This is the first entrée I made to impress my father-in-law. He fills the evening with heartfelt toasts and nostalgic stories. He's a larger-than-life character with a larger-than-life appetite. No matter what's on his plate he loves to mix it all together. I love making this dish for him because each bite is pre-assembled. Enjoy, Bruce!

3 tablespoons extra-virgin olive oil, divided

3 shallots, chopped

1½ pounds spinach, rinsed and chopped

½ cup dried cranberries

1½ cups low-sodium turkey or chicken broth, divided

¼ cup pine nuts, toasted

½ cup bread crumbs

½ cup pecorino cheese, freshly grated

One 2-pound turkey breast, boneless and skinless (ask your butcher to butterfly)

¼ pound prosciutto, thinly sliced

Kosher salt and freshly ground black pepper, to taste

½ cup dry white wine

1½ tablespoons butter

2 teaspoons freshly squeezed lemon juice

Kitchen twine

Pour 2 tablespoons of the olive oil in a large deep skillet over medium heat. Add the shallots and sauté, stirring frequently, until lightly golden.

Add the spinach and cook, stirring frequently, until spinach begins to wilt. Add the cranberries and ½ cup of the broth. Increase the heat to high and cook until most of the liquid evaporates. Remove from the heat and stir in the pine nuts, bread crumbs, and pecorino cheese. Set aside.

Open up the butterflied turkey breast and lay it on a piece of plastic wrap, allowing for several extra inches of wrap on either side. Cover turkey with another piece of plastic wrap. Pound breast with a meat mallet or a small heavy saucepan until it is an even thickness, about ½ inch thick. Discard top layer of plastic wrap.

Arrange the prosciutto in overlapping layers over the turkey. Spoon the spinach mixture evenly over the prosciutto. Roll up the turkey, making sure to discard the bottom sheet of plastic wrap. With seam side down, tie with kitchen twine about every inch crosswise and once lengthwise. Sprinkle with salt and pepper.

Pour the remaining oil in a large skillet over high heat until oil is very hot but not smoking. Cook turkey until nicely browned on all sides.

Add wine and the remaining broth. Reduce to low heat and cover the skillet. Let the turkey braise for 45 minutes, turning halfway through cooking.

(continued)

Once cooked, transfer the turkey to a carving board to rest. Tent loosely with aluminum foil.

Pour braising liquid through a fine-mesh sieve into a medium saucepan. Bring to a boil over high heat and cook until the liquid has reduced to about ½ cup. Reduce to low heat and stir in butter. Remove from heat and stir in lemon juice. If sauce needs a bit of thickening, feel free to whisk in a pinch of cornstarch.

Remove kitchen twine from the rested turkey and cut into 1-inch-thick slices. Drizzle with sauce and serve.

⌐ Stuff and roll your turkey breast the day before. Just wrap well in plastic wrap and refrigerate! When you're ready to cook, take your turkey out of the fridge and let it sit at room temperature for about 30 minutes before cooking.

New York steak with herb butter

SERVES 2

If the way to a man's heart is through his stomach, a steak is the easiest route to take. Traditionally people love the ritual of throwing steaks on a grill, but cooking the steak in a pan allows the steak to cook in its own juices. The herb butter is a quintessential accoutrement. Cook it this way and you will leave the steak sauce in the fridge.

Two 8-ounce New York steaks, (room temperature)

Kosher salt and freshly ground black pepper, to taste

2 teaspoons (or more) Herb Butter

2 teaspoons extra-virgin olive oil

Sprinkle the steaks generously with coarse salt and pepper. Melt 2 teaspoons herb butter with the oil in a cast-iron skillet or other heavy, medium skillet over medium-high heat until hot and almost smoking. Add the steaks to the skillet and cook to desired doneness, 3 to 4 minutes per side for medium-rare, turning only once. Transfer the steak to a plate; tent with aluminum foil and let rest for 5 minutes. If desired, top with an additional pat of herb butter.

Herb Butter

MAKES ½ CUP

8 tablespoons (1 stick) unsalted butter, softened to room temperature

½ teaspoon minced fresh chives

½ teaspoon minced fresh parsley

½ teaspoon minced fresh thyme

½ teaspoon minced fresh sage

¼ teaspoon (heaping) sea salt

Combine all the ingredients in a small bowl. Mix with a fork or silicone spatula until well blended.

Place a sheet of plastic wrap or parchment paper on the work surface. Transfer the butter mixture to the center of the plastic wrap. Fold one long side of the plastic wrap over the butter. Form the butter into a smooth and even log, about 1 to 1¼ inches in diameter, then enclose completely in the plastic wrap. The herb butter can be prepared ahead. Refrigerate or freeze.

"I have no special talent.

I am only passionately curious."

—Albert Einstein

Ricotta meatballs with chianti sauce

SERVES 4

I cook meatballs a bit differently. I don't fry them! Frying makes the meatballs so heavy and they always seem to break apart. Instead, I bake them to seal in the flavor and then finish the cooking in the red sauce. The ricotta cheese keeps them really moist, and the fennel seeds make the flavors pop. They. Are. Delicious. This is the dish I make the most.

SAUCE

½ cup finely minced onions

¼ cup extra-virgin olive oil

3 garlic cloves, peeled and minced

2 ounces prosciutto, finely diced

½ cup dry red wine

One 28-ounce can crushed San Marzano tomatoes

1 cup beef broth

MEATBALLS

1 pound lean ground beef

1 pound ground pork

1 cup fresh bread crumbs

½ cup fresh parsley, chopped

⅔ cup ricotta cheese

2 large eggs, beaten

2 teaspoons fennel seeds

1 teaspoon cumin

1 teaspoon dried chili flakes

1 teaspoon Kosher salt

1 teaspoon freshly ground black pepper

Parmigiano-Reggiano wedge

To make the Chianti Sauce: sauté minced onions in extra-virgin olive oil for 5 minutes, add 3 cloves of garlic and the prosciutto and continue to sauté for 1 more minute. Add ½ cup wine and cook for 1 minute. Add the crushed tomatoes and beef broth and simmer for 30 minutes.

To make the meatballs: Preheat oven to 450°F. Lightly spray a baking sheet with cooking oil spray. Place all the ingredients in a large bowl and mix together by hand. Roll your meatballs, making 2-inch balls. Place them on the prepared baking sheet and bake for 10 minutes.

Remove the meatballs from the oven and add them to your Chianti sauce. Simmer for 15 minutes or until cooked through. Serve the meatballs with the cheese wedge and a grater on the table for your guests.

Substitute ground turkey for the beef and pork for a lighter meatball option.

Cauliflower-reggiano puree

MAKES ABOUT 4 CUPS

*This recipe will surprise you. The cauliflower has a luxurious smooth
texture, and takes on the flavor of the Reggiano. This is a great low-carb
substitute for mashed potatoes and a staple side dish for my family. It's
wonderful served with pretty much every entrée in Cooking School.*

4½ cups cauliflower florets
(from about 2 heads cauliflower)

½ cup (or more) vegetable
broth

¼ cup finely grated
Parmigiano-Reggiano
cheese

1 tablespoon unsalted butter

¼ teaspoon sea salt

¼ teaspoon freshly ground
black pepper

Chopped fresh chives
(optional)

Combine the cauliflower florets and ½ cup vegetable broth in a heavy
medium saucepan. Bring to a boil. Reduce the heat to medium-low;
cover and simmer until the cauliflower is very tender, stirring occasionally, and adding more broth by tablespoonfuls to moisten if broth
cooks away, about 15 minutes.

Transfer the mixture to a food processor. Add the cheese, butter,
salt, and pepper; puree until smooth, adding more broth, if needed,
for desired consistency. Transfer the puree to a serving bowl. Sprinkle
with chives, if desired.

German chocolate cupcakes

48 MINI CUPCAKES

Years ago when I was single, I had no plans for Valentine's Day. My friend Tracy and I baked cupcakes and delivered them to all the broken hearts in our lives. It was an unforgettable day! I've always loved a cupcake—especially these with a gooey coconut frosting. Yum. These are inspired by the Queen of baking, Martha Stewart.

CUPCAKES

7 ounces sweetened dark chocolate, chopped

2 cups flour

1 teaspoon baking soda

¾ teaspoon sea salt

12 tablespoons (1½ sticks) unsalted butter, softened

1½ cups sugar

3 large eggs, room temperature

2 teaspoons vanilla extract

1 cup buttermilk

FROSTING

3 large egg yolks

12 tablespoons (1½ sticks) unsalted butter, softened

One 14-ounce can sweetened condensed milk

½ cup packed brown sugar

7 ounces sweetened flaked coconut

6 ounces toasted pecans, coarsely chopped

1 teaspoon vanilla extract

¼ teaspoon sea salt

To make the cupcakes: Position the rack in the center of the oven and preheat the oven to 350°F. Line a mini muffin pan with mini muffin paper liners. Melt the chocolate in a double boiler over low heat until just melted and smooth. Set aside to cool slightly while making the batter.

Combine the flour, baking soda, and salt in a medium bowl; whisk to blend.

Using an electric mixer, beat the butter and sugar in a large bowl until fluffy. Add the eggs, one at a time, beating until blended after each addition. Beat in the vanilla. Add the flour mixture alternately with the buttermilk in three additions each and beat just until blended. Add the melted chocolate and beat until incorporated and smooth. Spoon the batter into the prepared mini muffin pans, filling the cups ¾ full. Bake the cupcakes until a tester inserted in the center comes out clean, about 10 minutes. Transfer the pan to a rack and cool the cupcakes completely.

For the frosting: Combine the egg yolks, butter, condensed milk, and sugar in a heavy medium saucepan. Stir over medium-low heat until thickened, about 10 minutes. Transfer the mixture to a medium bowl. Add the coconut, pecans, vanilla, and salt and stir to blend well. Cool the frosting completely. Spread the frosting on top of the cupcakes and serve. (See page 116 for photo.)

Savoring the last bites of summer

Imagine this: It's two o'clock in the afternoon on a Sunday in September. Everyone is settling back into their routine life after their summer adventures. Why not reconnect with friends in person while capturing the last bounty of the season? Enjoy the summery tastes of shrimp, mint, and melons while cooking jams and chutneys together to last through the colder seasons. Serve with crusty artisan breads and butter.

PARTY OF 6

Agua Fresca **25**

Shrimp with Feta and Mint **26**

Strawberry-Rhubarb Jam **28**

Balsamic Fig Chutney **29**

Agua fresca

SERVES 6

This recipe is a Latin American treat. It's an incredibly refreshing summer drink that uses very ripe cantaloupes, honeydews, or watermelons. Thirst quenching.

Cheesecloth

4 cups peeled, seeded, cubed ripe cantaloupe (from 1 medium cantaloupe)

2 cups water

¼ cup loosely packed basil leaves

3 tablespoons fresh lime juice

2½ teaspoons agave syrup

Ice cubes

Set a large strainer over a large bowl. Line the strainer with the cheesecloth. Combine 2 cups cantaloupe, 1 cup water, 2 tablespoons basil, 1½ tablespoons lime juice, and 1¼ teaspoons agave syrup in a blender. Blend on high until the mixture is as smooth as possible. Pour the mixture into the cheesecloth-lined strainer, pressing gently on the solids to extract as much liquid as possible. Repeat with the remaining cantaloupe, water, basil, lime juice, and agave. Discard the solids in the strainer.

Pour the cantaloupe agua fresca into a pitcher, add enough ice cubes to chill the drink, and serve over ice.

Shrimp with feta and mint

SERVES 6

This recipe is inspired by a dish from an old L.A. restaurant called Pane Vino. It's long closed, but I couldn't forget these flavors. The best part is soaking up the minty lime juices with a crusty baguette.

¼ cup dry white wine

Juice from 1 lemon

1 tablespoon plus 5 tablespoons extra-virgin olive oil, divided

24 large shrimp (about 1¼ pounds), peeled, deveined, with tails attached

1 cup fresh mint leaves, loosely packed

½ cup feta cheese, crumbled

4 limes, halved

Sourdough baguette

Sea salt and freshly ground black pepper, to taste

Pour wine, lemon juice, and 1 tablespoon olive oil in a large skillet and bring to a boil over high heat. Reduce heat so that mixture is at a simmer.

Working in batches, add eight shrimp at a time to cooking liquid and simmer for about 4 minutes, turning after 2 minutes. When shrimp is done, it will have turned a bright pink. Be careful not to overcook.

Transfer shrimp to a bowl with a slotted spoon. Set aside the cooking liquid. Let shrimp cool for 5 minutes. Cover and refrigerate for one hour.

Place reserved cooking liquid in a small bowl and refrigerate.

To serve, scatter the mint on a large platter. Arrange shrimp on the mint and sprinkle with the feta cheese. Squeeze juice from the limes over the shrimp and drizzle with the remaining olive oil and cooled cooking liquid. Toss lightly to mix flavors. Place the baguette around the shrimp, and give the dish a dash of salt and a couple of twists of freshly cracked pepper. You're ready to serve!

Strawberry-rhubarb jam

MAKES APPROXIMATELY 3 CUPS

Rhubarb is a tough one to figure out. It looks like red celery and has a horrible-sounding name. But don't be too quick to judge. What I like about this underdog is that it compliments this sweet chunky strawberry jam with a tart freshness.

3 cups hulled sliced fresh strawberries, divided

3 cups thinly sliced fresh rhubarb

3½ teaspoons fresh lemon juice

1½ cups sugar

Combine 1½ cups of the strawberries and all of the rhubarb in a large bowl. Drizzle the lemon juice over the berries and rhubarb and sprinkle with the sugar. Toss to blend. Let stand at room temperature until juices form, at least 30 minutes.

Transfer the fruit mixture to a heavy medium saucepan. Bring to a boil, stirring occasionally until the sugar dissolves. Reduce the heat to medium and cook, covered, until the mixture thickens slightly, stirring often to prevent sticking, about 15 minutes. Add the remaining 1½ cups strawberries to the simmering fruit mixture and cook for 3 minutes longer. Remove from the heat and allow the jam to cool slightly in the pan, about 15 minutes.

Stir the jam and transfer to a container. Cool completely. Cover and refrigerate or freeze up to 6 months.

Balsamic fig chutney

I love figs, the way they look and taste. They are a splurge. Fortunately, they grow abundantly in California, and my neighbor lets me steal them from her tree. This chutney is so versatile; you can use it on practically anything, from sandwiches, to charcuterie plates, to any meats. It freezes well and will last a long time, so don't be afraid to double the recipe and stock up.

1 tablespoon whole coriander seed

2 cinnamon sticks

4 cups quartered fresh figs (about 1½ pounds)

¾ cup dry white wine

⅔ cup minced shallot

½ cup balsamic vinegar

½ cup firmly packed dark brown sugar

2 teaspoons finely grated peeled fresh ginger

Stir the coriander and cinnamon sticks in a heavy two-quart saucepan over medium-high heat until the spices are toasted and fragrant, about 1 minute. Immediately add the remaining ingredients. Reduce heat to medium-low and cook, covered, stirring occasionally, until the chutney is thickened to a jamlike consistency, about 30 minutes.

Transfer the chutney to jars, cool completely. Cover and refrigerate or freeze up to 6 months.

⌐ **Canned figs or fresh plums are a great year-round alternative.**

october

Harvest party

The season has changed and fall is upon us. The brisk air makes me crave hardier and richer flavors. My harvest party is a plated sit-down dinner. A lot of the recipes for this party require some time, so think of it as playing in the kitchen—braising, peeling, and baking. Enjoy it. This is a chance to invite over your boyfriend's parents, impress your boss, or is just a great excuse to spend the day cooking while listening to Billie Holiday.

PARTY OF 8

Butternut Squash Soup with Crispy Sage 35

Kale Salad with Pecorino and Truffle Vinaigrette 36

Braised Short Ribs with Balsamic Vinegar 39

Apple Crostata with Aged Gouda 40

Butternut squash soup with crispy sage

SERVES 6

This thick soup really makes the squash shine and is very simple to make. Depending on how fancy I'm feeling, I will either serve it as a first course in hollowed mini pumpkins or leave it simmering on the stove and let friends fill mugs.

SERVING OPTION

1 to 3 small sugar pumpkins for serving

SOUP

6 cups 1-inch pieces peeled, seeded butternut squash (approximately 3 pounds pre-cut squash)

3 cups vegetable broth, or more

¾ cup half and half

¾ teaspoon dried sage

¾ teaspoon sea salt

¾ teaspoon freshly ground black pepper

1½ tablespoons unsalted butter

8 sage leaves

To make the pumpkin bowl: Preheat the oven to 350°F. Cut the pumpkins crosswise into even halves (these will be used as bowls for the soup). Scrape out the seeds and toast for the kale salad. Place the pumpkin halves, cut side up, on a rimmed baking sheet. Bake for 20 minutes. Remove from the oven and let the pumpkins cool on the baking sheet.

To make the soup: Place the squash in a large pot. Add the vegetable broth. Bring to a boil. Reduce the heat, cover, and simmer until the squash is tender, 10 to 15 minutes. Remove from the heat and cool slightly. Transfer the squash and vegetable broth to a food processor and puree until smooth. Return the squash to the same pot. Add the half and half, dried sage, salt, pepper, and additional broth if needed, and bring to a simmer over medium-low heat until heated through, about 5 minutes. Serve with sage leaves on top.

To make the crispy sage leaves: Heat butter in a medium skillet over medium heat. Add sage leaves and a pinch of salt. Sauté until crispy, about 1 minute each side.

↪ **To make this soup vegan substitute more broth for the half and half. Add a pureed apple to the butternut squash to pump up the flavor.**

Kale salad with pecorino and truffle vinaigrette

SERVES 6

It's funny how certain foods become popular, and kale is definitely the "it-girl" of the season. She's hearty, wholesome, and a great co-star to braised beef. Kale is also packed with nutrients good for both body and soul. The truffle vinaigrette is simple and special.

VINAIGRETTE

¼ cup extra-virgin olive oil

1 tablespoon truffle oil

1 tablespoon fresh lemon juice, or more to taste

¼ teaspoon truffle salt

¼ teaspoon freshly ground black pepper

SALAD

6 cups thinly sliced fresh kale, center ribs removed

6 tablespoons finely grated Pecorino cheese

6 tablespoons dried cranberries

½ cup toasted pumpkin seeds

To make the vinaigrette: Whisk all the ingredients in a small bowl to blend.

To make the salad: Toss the kale with the vinaigrette in a large bowl. Sprinkle the cheese, cranberries, and pumpkin seeds over the kale and serve.

Substitute all extra-virgin olive oil for the truffle oil for a less expensive lemon vinaigrette.

Braised Short ribs with balsamic vinegar

SERVES 6

There are a few tricks to make these short ribs a cut above the rest. A double reduction—reducing the wine to a glaze and then reducing the final sauce before serving—brings depth of flavor. Also, the balsamic vinegar brings a tangy sweetness. I'm a sucker for a dinner party dish that you can prepare the night before.

1 bottle zinfandel wine

12 meaty beef short ribs, about 5–6 pounds

2 teaspoons kosher salt

2 teaspoons freshly ground black pepper

1½ tablespoons extra-virgin olive oil

2 cups chopped onions

2 cups chopped celery

2 cups chopped carrots

6 large garlic cloves, chopped

2 tablespoons chopped fresh thyme

4 teaspoons chopped fresh rosemary

2 tablespoons all purpose flour

2 Turkish bay leaves

3 tablespoons balsamic vinegar

32 ounces beef broth

In a large pot, rapidly boil down wine for 10 minutes, reducing it to approximately 1 cup. Set aside.

Preheat the oven to 325°F. Sprinkle the short ribs with 2 teaspoons salt and 2 teaspoons pepper all over. Heat the oil in a large deep oven-proof pot over high heat. Working in batches, add the short ribs to the pot and sear until brown on all sides, 2 minutes per batch. Transfer the ribs to a bowl.

Add the onions, celery, and carrots to the same pot and sauté until tender and golden, about 10 minutes. Add the garlic, thyme, and rosemary; stir 1 minute. Stir in flour and mix thoroughly. Add the bay leaves, wine, vinegar and beef broth simmer 2 to 3 minutes. Return the short ribs to the pot, bring to boil. Cover the pot tightly with a lid. Place the pot in the oven and braise until the ribs are very tender and almost fall of the bones, 2½ hours. Remove the pot from the oven. Cool, cover, and refrigerate overnight.

Remove ribs from refrigerator and discard the majority of the fat that will have solidified on the top. Remove ribs from sauce and place in a bowl. Strain the sauce through a sieve, into a large bowl, pressing on the solids. Return juices to pot on stove. Bring the pan juices in the pot to boil. Simmer the juices until thickened to desired sauce consistency, about 30 minutes. Season the sauce lightly to taste with salt and pepper. Return the ribs to the pot and simmer until heated through, about 5 minutes. Devour!

Apple crostata with aged gouda

SERVES 6 TO 8

When I first started pursuing my dream of being an actress, my mom would drive me two hours each way to my auditions in New York City. On top of doing her own work and keeping the family connected, she somehow found the time to bake. Her sweet and savory Down Under Apple Pie was always a family favorite. I gave it my own twist by using sharp, aged gouda and making it a mistake-free crostata. Enjoy!

CRUST

1½ cups all purpose flour

3 tablespoons sugar

¾ teaspoon kosher salt

12 tablespoons (1½ sticks) chilled unsalted butter, cut into ½-inch cubes

3 tablespoons (or more) ice water

FILLING

3 to 4 apples, peeled, cored, quartered, and thinly sliced, about 3 cups (I like Granny Smith.)

¼ cup sugar

2 tablespoons all-purpose flour

½ teaspoon ground cinnamon

½ teaspoon sea salt

½ teaspoon finely grated lemon zest

¼ cup (½ stick) chilled, unsalted butter, cut into ½-inch cubes

½ cup coarsely grated aged Gouda cheese

To make the crust: Blend the flour, sugar, and salt in a food processor. Add the butter and pulse using on/off turns until the mixture resembles coarse meal. Add 3 tablespoons ice water through the feed tube and blend just until moist clumps form, adding more ice water by teaspoonfuls if the dough is dry. Dough can be prepared 1 day ahead. Keep refrigerated. (Chill dough for 10 minutes before rolling.)

Using floured hands or a rolling pin, push out the dough disk on lightly floured parchment paper, forming a 12-inch round. Transfer the parchment paper with the crust to a large rimmed baking sheet. Chill the dough while preparing the filling.

To make the filling: Position the rack in the center of the oven and preheat to 375°F. Combine the apples, sugar, flour, cinnamon, salt, and lemon zest in a medium bowl; toss to blend. Stir in the butter pieces. Mound the apple filling in the center of the rolled-out dough round, leaving 1½-inch plain border. Gently fold the dough border up over the apple filling, forming a rim, and pleating the dough edge as needed. Pinch any cracks together with your fingers. Sprinkle the Gouda cheese over the top of the filling.

Bake the crostata until apples are tender and crust is crisp and golden, 30 to 35 minutes. Run a long sharp knife under the crostata to loosen it from the parchment and to prevent sticking. Slide a flat pan bottom under the crostata and transfer to a serving plate. Cut into wedges and serve slightly warm, with a dollop of crème fraîche if desired.

Full moon party

Cultures all over the world celebrate the full moon. The full moon always seems to bring out mischievousness. So why not make a party of it? Invite over friends, cook up some chili, and go for a nighttime walk in the brisk air while sipping spiked hot chocolate.

PARTY OF 6

Oak Leaf Lettuces with Balsamic Vinaigrette 44

Lagered Turkey Chili 45

Jalapeño Cheddar Cornbread with Maple Syrup Drizzle 47

Spiked Hot Chocolate 48

Oak leaf lettuces with balsamic vinaigrette

SERVES 6

I spent a year mad at balsamic vinegar, because I thought it was so strong and overpowered everything. But it is back in my good graces when balanced right. This is a flavorful vinaigrette that is lovely with heartier dishes.

5 tablespoons extra-virgin olive oil

1 tablespoon fresh lemon juice

1 tablespoon balsamic vinegar

¼ teaspoon sea salt

¼ teaspoon freshly ground black pepper

6 cups oak leaf lettuce

Whisk olive oil, lemon juice, and vinegar in a small bowl until emulsified. Season the vinaigrette to taste with salt and pepper.

Place the lettuce in a large bowl. Add the dressing and toss to coat.

Lagered turkey chili

This is one of my go-to dishes—fuss free but full of flavor. Sometimes I indulge by substituting in grass-fed ground beef. Either way, the chocolate and Guinness make it an amazing chili that people adore. Serve with sour cream, grated Cheddar cheese, and sliced green onions.

3 tablespoons chili powder

2 tablespoons ground cumin

½ teaspoon dried red chili flakes

¼ cup extra-virgin olive oil

3 cups chopped onion (from about 2 medium)

2 cups chopped seeded green bell peppers (from about 2)

6 garlic cloves, peeled and minced

2 pounds ground turkey meat, white or dark

1 tablespoon dried oregano

2 tablespoons tomato paste

1 tablespoon sea salt

1 tablespoon cocoa powder or 1 ounce dark chocolate, chopped

One 12-ounce bottle Guinness or lager beer

One 14½-ounce can diced tomatoes

Two 15½-ounce cans kidney beans, rinsed and drained

Mix the chili powder, cumin, and chili flakes in a small bowl. Heat a heavy large nonstick pot over medium-high heat. Add the chili powder mixture to the pot and stir for 30 seconds to 1 minute until fragrant.

Add the oil to the pot, then add the onions, bell peppers, and garlic and sauté until beginning to soften, about 5 minutes. Add the turkey and sauté until no longer pink, about 5 minutes. Add the oregano, then the tomato paste, salt, and cocoa powder; stir 1 minute. Add the beer and simmer 5 minutes. Add the diced tomatoes and the beans. Bring to a boil. Reduce the heat to medium-low and simmer slighty covered until the flavors develop, about 30 minutes. Serve with Jalapeño cornbread.

Jalapeño cheddar cornbread with maple syrup drizzle

SERVES 6 TO 8

This cornbread is as quick and flavorful as it gets. Mix up the ingredients, melt some butter in a a cast-iron pan, throw in the batter and watch it sizzle. Drizzling with maple syrup makes the cornbread savory sweet. Voilà, a crowd-pleaser.

1 cup cornmeal

1 cup all-purpose flour

½ teaspoon sea salt

½ teaspoon baking soda

1 cup whole milk

2 large eggs

1 tablespoon fresh lemon juice

1 tablespoon plus ¼ cup pure maple syrup, divided

1 cup coarsely grated sharp Cheddar cheese

¼ cup seeded chopped jalapeños (from about 3 jalapeños)

1½ tablespoons butter

1½ tablespoons extra-virgin olive oil

Position the rack in the center of the oven and preheat to 425°F. Whisk the cornmeal, flour, salt, and baking soda in a medium bowl to blend. In another medium bowl, whisk the milk, eggs, lemon juice, and 1 tablespoon maple syrup until well blended. Add the milk mixture to the flour mixture and stir to incorporate. Stir in cheese and the jalapeños.

Melt the butter with the olive oil in a 10-inch cast-iron skillet or other ovenproof skillet over medium-high heat. Pour the cornmeal batter into the skillet. It will sizzle. Transfer the skillet to the oven and bake the cornbread in the hot skillet for 15–20 minutes, until lightly golden. Remove the skillet from the oven and cool the cornbread slightly in the skillet. Use toothpicks or a cake-tester to puncture little holes in the top and drizzle the remaining ¼ cup maple syrup so that it soaks the cornbread. Cut the cornbread into wedges and serve.

You can also bake the cornbread in a muffin tin.

Spiked hot chocolate

SERVES 6

This hot chocolate is a rich, decadent sip. Spike it if you please.

6 cups whole milk

9 ounces premium dark chocolate, chopped

6 tablespoons packed dark
brown sugar

1½ teaspoons vanilla extract

6 shots of rum, whiskey, or
añejo tequila

Softly whipped cream (see
page 68)

Combine the milk, chocolate, and brown sugar in a medium saucepan. Heat over medium heat until the chocolate melts and the sugar dissolves, stirring occasionally. Remove the saucepan from the heat and stir in the vanilla.

Pour the hot chocolate in each mug. Add a shot of liquor. Top each with a large dollop of whipped cream and serve.

"Twenty years from now you'll be more disappointed

by the things you didn't do than

by the ones you did do. . . ."

—Mark Twain

november

Out-of-town guests

Many out-of-town guests show up at our doorstep throughout the holiday season. I love to wake them up to the smell of muffins baking while I'm still in my pajamas. Have your guests sit down to a cup of freshly brewed coffee with all the newspapers and a stack of unread *New Yorkers*. Start a fire, play some Cole Porter, and allow them to relax into the day. Then slay them with these extraordinary eggs. Serve with a big bowl of berries, greek yogurt, and slivered mint.

PARTY OF 4

Carrot Ginger Muffins 54

Skillet Eggs with Smoked Bacon and Spinach 55

Espresso Affogato 55

Carrot ginger muffins

MAKES 12 MUFFINS

I love these earthy muffins. They balance out the richness of the eggs. I feel good about feeding them to my family, and they always surprise my friends with their guilt-free ingredients. I don't ever make anything just because it's healthy. I make things because they are delicious, and this one just happens to be healthy.

1½ cups spelt or whole-wheat flour

⅓ cup wheat germ

¼ cup ground flax seeds

4 teaspoons ground cinnamon

3 teaspoons baking powder

1½ teaspoons baking soda

½ teaspoon ground cloves

½ teaspoon sea salt

¾ cup agave syrup

3 small eggs

6 tablespoons extra-virgin olive oil

2 teaspoons vanilla extract

1½ teaspoons finely grated peeled fresh ginger

2 cups finely grated carrots

¾ cup pecans, chopped, additional 12 whole pecans if you want to put one on top of each muffin

Additional agave syrup, for drizzling

Flaked sea salt, to taste

Position the rack in the center of the oven and preheat to 400°F. Line a 12-cup standard muffin pan with paper liners. Whisk flour, wheat germ, ground flax seeds, cinnamon, baking powder, baking soda, cloves, and salt in a large bowl to blend. Whisk agave, eggs, olive oil, vanilla, and fresh ginger in a medium bowl to blend. Add the agave mixture to the dry ingredients and stir gently just until incorporated. Fold in the grated carrots and pecans.

Divide the batter equally among the 12 muffin cups, filling the cups to the top. Bake the muffins until a tester inserted into the center of a muffin comes out clean, 20 to 22 minutes. Transfer the muffin pan to a rack and let cool slightly before serving. Drizzle with additional agave and flaked sea salt. (See page 56 for photo.)

Skillet eggs with smoked bacon and spinach

SERVES 4

People fawn over the bacony croutons with fresh eggs. This dish is inspired by Jean-Georges Vongerichten's fried eggs. I like to buy farmer's-market eggs and organic bacon. Feel free to use any veggies you have on hand, or substitute the bacon with sausage.

8 thick-cut smoked bacon slices, cut into 1-inch pieces

2 cups sourdough bread cubes with crust

1 tablespoon thinly sliced shallot

1½ cups packed baby spinach leaves

8 large eggs

2 tablespoons chopped fresh chives

Freshly ground black pepper and sea salt, to taste

Cook the bacon in a large nonstick skillet over medium-low heat until cooked halfway through, 5 to 7 minutes. Add the sourdough cubes and shallot to the skillet and sauté until the bread is golden brown in spots, 2 to 4 minutes, pressing down to form a crust. Scatter the spinach over the bread mixture and then crack the eggs over the mixture in the skillet. Cover the skillet and cook the eggs until the whites are set but the yolks are still runny, 2 to 3 minutes. You may need to gently move around the egg whites to ensure even cooking. Sprinkle the eggs with chives, freshly cracked black pepper, and sea salt. Serve right from the pan, cutting out slices, family style. (See page 57 for photo.)

Espresso affogato

SERVES 4

This espresso dessert is a fun wonderful treat after a meal. Hey, you put cream and sugar in your coffee anyway, right?

4 scoops vanilla ice cream

8 shots hot espresso

Place 1 small scoop of vanilla ice cream each in 4 small glasses. Serve 2 hot espresso shots in a small cup alongside each glass. Have guests pour the espresso over the ice cream. (See page 52 for photo.)

Friends Thanksgiving

Thanksgiving dinner with family is fun, Thanksgiving dinner with friends is a blast. Hayes and I had been married a year, and his family was coming to spend the holiday with us. It was up to me to host my first Thanksgiving! As a trial run, a week before the actual big day, I hosted a "Thanksgiving" for all my friends. Friends Thanksgiving became a demanded annual event. There were no family stresses and this raucous party ended up with everyone stuffed and imbibed. Be forewarned. Scotch Guard your couch against red wine because revelrous behavior is destined to break out.

PARTY OF 12 TO 16

Butternut Squash Soup with Crispy Sage (see page 35)

Kale Salad with Pecorino and Truffle Vinaigrette (see page 36)

Herb-Buttered Turkey with Clementine 61

Buttermilk Mashed Potatoes 63

Rustic Sausage and Fennel Stuffing 64

Green Bean Casserole with Wild Mushrooms 66

Pumpkin Pie with Gingersnap Cookie Crust 68

Herb-buttered turkey with clementine

SERVES 12 TO 16

This is the king of the meal. First and foremost, don't be intimidated. It is really hard to mess up, and the oohs and ahhs you'll hear will be well worth your love and time. Brining is essential and is worth the small amount of time, but be sure to start 24 hours in advance. I post a time-chart of the entire meal to stay organized. The herb butter with clementine and the wine in the gravy really make this special.

TURKEY STOCK

3 tablespoons unsalted butter

2 pounds turkey necks and/or wings

3 cups chopped unpeeled onions (from about 2 large)

1 cup chopped scrubbed carrots (from about 2 large)

1 cup chopped celery

4 garlic cloves, unpeeled

6 cups (or more) low-salt chicken broth

5 cups water

HERB BUTTER

16 tablespoons (2 sticks) unsalted butter, softened

½ cup extra-virgin olive oil

½ cup chopped fresh parsley

2 tablespoons chopped shallot (from about 1 small)

2 tablespoons chopped fresh chives

To make the turkey stock: Melt the butter in a heavy large stockpot over high heat. Add the turkey necks and/or wings and cook until deep brown, 7 to 8 minutes per side. Add the onions, carrots, celery, and garlic; sauté until the vegetables are brown, about 12 minutes. Add 6 cups chicken broth and 5 cups water and bring to a boil. Reduce the heat; cover partially, and simmer for 1 hour, stirring occasionally.

Discard the turkey necks and/or wings. Strain the stock through a sieve into a large bowl, pressing on the solids in the sieve to extract as much liquid as possible. If necessary, add enough chicken broth to the turkey stock to measure 8½ cups total. (The turkey stock can be prepared ahead. Cool. Cover and keep chilled for up to 2 days, or pour into a freezer container and freeze for up to 1 month. Rewarm before using.)

To make the herb butter: Combine all the herb-butter ingredients in a small bowl and mix with a fork or silicone spatula until well blended.

To make the turkey brine: Combine 1 gallon water, sugar, salt, parsley, sage, thyme, and peppercorns in a large pot. Bring to a boil, stirring occasionally to dissolve the sugar and salt. Reduce the heat and simmer for 10 minutes. Cool the brine completely. (The brine can be prepared 2 days ahead. Cover and refrigerate. Bring to room temperature before using.)

(continued)

2 tablespoons chopped fresh
   sage

2 tablespoons chopped fresh
   thyme

2 large garlic cloves, peeled and
   chopped

2 tablespoons fresh clementine
   juice

1 teaspoon finely grated clementine zest

TURKEY BRINE

1 gallon water

1½ cups sugar

1½ cups kosher salt

½ bunch fresh parsley

One 1-ounce package fresh
   sage sprigs

One 1-ounce package fresh
   thyme sprigs

3 tablespoons whole black peppercorns

1 food-grade brining bag (available at butchers and some
   supermarkets)

One 18-pound organic turkey,
   rinsed inside and out, patted dry

Place the brining bag in a large container or a cooler and place the turkey in the bag. Pour the brine into the bag over the turkey, adding enough cold water to the bag to fully submerge the turkey. Seal the bag tightly and refrigerate the turkey, or keep the turkey in a cooler filled with ice for 24 hours.

For the turkey and gravy: One hour before roasting, take the turkey out of the brine. Rinse the turkey inside and out with cold water; pat dry.

Position the rack in the bottom third of the oven and preheat to 425°F. Scatter the chopped vegetables in a large roasting pan. Pour 1½ cups of the turkey stock into the roasting pan. Place the turkey, breast side up, on a rack in the roasting pan. Place any leftover herbs, clementines, and 4 tablespoons herb butter in the main cavity of the turkey. Tuck the wing tips under the turkey and tie the legs together to hold shape. Starting at the neck end of the turkey, carefully slide your hand between the skin and breast meat to loosen the skin. Rub 4 tablespoons herb butter over the breast meat under the skin. Rub 4 tablespoons herb butter over the outside of the turkey. Sprinkle the turkey generously with salt and pepper.

Roast the turkey 20 minutes. Reduce the oven temperature to 350°F. Continue roasting the turkey until an instant-read thermometer inserted into the thickest part of the thigh registers 175°F, basting every 30 minutes with the juices from the roasting pan and adding more broth to the roasting pan as needed, 3 to 3½ hours total. Tent the turkey with foil halfway through roasting if browning too quickly.

Remove the turkey from the roasting pan and tent with foil completely. Rest for 30 minutes before carving.

Meanwhile, to make the gravy: Pour the turkey pan juices through a sieve into a bowl. Place the empty roasting pan over 2 stove-top burners. Melt the remaining 4 tablespoons herb butter in the roasting pan over medium heat. Add the flour and whisk constantly to make a roux for the gravy, about 3 minutes (the mixture will be thick). Add

(continued)

TURKEY AND GRAVY

2 onions, sliced

6 celery stalks, chopped

4 carrots, peeled, chopped

2 clementines, quartered (use the remainder of 1 clementine from the herb butter recipe)

½ cup all purpose flour

1¼ cups dry white wine

the wine and bring to a boil, whisking constantly until smooth, 3 to 4 minutes. Gradually pour in the remaining 7 cups turkey stock and bring to a boil, whisking constantly until smooth and slightly thickened, about 5 minutes. Reduce the heat and simmer until the gravy is reduced and thickened to a desired consistency, whisking occasionally, about 15 minutes longer. Season the gravy to taste with salt and pepper.

Carve the turkey and serve with the gravy.

To make homemade cranberries, boil 2 cups water with 2 cups sugar. Add a package of cranberries, a bit of orange zest and simmer till berries burst. Chill.

Buttermilk mashed potatoes

SERVES 12 TO 16

Another staple at the Thanksgiving table, these mashed potatoes have a secret ingredient: baking soda. It's an unexpected addition that makes it the lightest, fluffiest mashed potato imaginable. Shhhh...

6 pounds russet potatoes, peeled, cut into 2-inch chunks

5 teaspoons sea salt, divided

8 tablespoons (1 stick) unsalted butter

1½ cups buttermilk

2 teaspoons baking soda

1 tablespoon freshly ground black pepper

Chopped fresh chives, for garnish

Place the potatoes in a large pot. Add enough cold water to cover by 2 inches. Add 1 teaspoon salt and bring to a boil. Reduce the heat to medium and boil gently until very tender when pierced with a fork, 25 to 30 minutes. Drain well. Return the potatoes to the pot.

Melt the butter in a small saucepan over medium-low heat. Remove from the heat. Stir in the buttermilk and baking soda. Using a handheld mixer or a potato masher, mix or mash the potatoes, then add the buttermilk mixture and mix until smooth. Season with pepper and the remaining salt. Transfer the mashed potatoes to a large bowl. Sprinkle with chives and salt and pepper to taste. Serve.

Rustic sausage and fennel stuffing

SERVES 12 TO 16

This stuffing may be my favorite side dish in the book. I love the combination of sausage with fragrant fennel. If you only make one dish this holiday season, make this the one. But don't blame me if you end up eating it again at midnight like I do.

12 cups 1-inch-cubed sourdough bread, crust on

3 tablespoons extra-virgin olive oil, divided

3 pounds organic sweet Italian sausages, casing removed

12 tablespoons (1½ sticks) unsalted butter

4½ cups chopped onions (from about 3 large)

3 cups chopped fresh fennel

9 garlic cloves, peeled and minced

1½ teaspoons kosher salt

1½ teaspoons freshly ground black pepper

6 large eggs, beaten to blend

1½ cups half and half, divided

1½ cups finely grated Parmigiano cheese

¾ cup low-salt chicken broth

¾ cup chopped fresh parsley

Preheat oven to 350. Spread the bread cubes in a single layer on 2 large rimmed baking sheets. Bake the bread cubes until lightly toasted, switching the positions of the baking sheets halfway through baking, 10 to 15 minutes total. Remove the bread cubes from the oven and set aside.

Heat 1½ tablespoons olive oil in a heavy large skillet over medium-high heat. Working in batches, add the sausages to the skillet and sauté until browned and cooked through, breaking up with back of fork or spoon, 5 to 7 minutes per batch. Transfer to a bowl large enough to hold the entire stuffing. (Do not clean the skillet).

Melt the butter in the same skillet over medium-high heat. Add the onions, fennel, garlic, salt, and pepper and sauté until the onions are golden brown, stirring frequently, 10 to 12 minutes. Transfer to the bowl with the sausage. Mix in the toasted bread cubes.

Whisk the eggs, 1 cup half and half, Parmesan, broth, and parsley in a medium bowl to blend. Pour the egg mixture over the sausage-and-bread mixture and toss gently to coat. Transfer the stuffing to two 9×9 baking pans. Drizzle the remaining ½ cup half and half over the stuffing.

Bake the stuffing, covered with foil, for 25 minutes. Remove the foil and bake uncovered until the top begins to brown, about 20 minutes longer.

Green bean casserole with wild mushrooms

SERVES 12 TO 16

This casserole is inspired by my friend Ike's version of the classic American green bean casserole. I sauté leeks and shallots for the "fried onion" topping, but feel free to buy the classic canned ones if you are a sucker for tradition. To me, there are no rules in cooking, except to cook what tastes good and what makes you feel good.

CREAM OF MUSHROOM SOUP

8 tablespoons (1 stick) unsalted butter, divided

1 cup finely chopped shallots (from 3 to 4 large)

3 large garlic cloves, peeled and chopped (for about 1 tablespoon)

2 pounds assorted mushrooms (such as crimini, portobella, and stemmed shiitake), coarsely chopped

1 tablespoon finely chopped fresh thyme

½ cup all-purpose flour

1 cup whole milk

2 cups heavy whipping cream

2 chicken bouillon cubes or vegetable bouillon cubes dissolved in 1 cup hot water

1 teaspoon kosher salt

1 teaspoon freshly ground black pepper

To make the cream of mushroom soup: Melt 4 tablespoons butter in a heavy large skillet or pot over medium-high heat. Add the shallots and sauté until slightly softened, 2 to 3 minutes. Add the garlic and stir 1 minute. Add the mushrooms and sauté until tender and browned, 8 to 10 minutes. Add the thyme and stir 1 minute. Remove from the heat.

Melt the remaining 4 tablespoons butter in a medium saucepan over medium heat. Add the flour and stir constantly, 1 to 2 minutes (the mixture will be very thick). Gradually add the milk, then cream and the dissolved bouillon mixture, whisking constantly until the mixture boils, thickens, and is smooth. Stir in the salt and pepper. Remove from the heat. Mix the mushrooms into the sauce; cover to keep warm.

To make the green bean casserole: Cook the beans in a large pot of boiling salted water until just crisp-tender, 2 to 3 minutes. Drain. Place the beans in large bowl of ice water to stop the cooking. When cool, drain the beans well.

Melt the butter with the olive oil in a heavy large skillet (preferably cast-iron) over medium-high heat. Add the leeks and shallots and sauté until tender and lightly golden (do not over-brown as the leeks will continue to brown in the oven), 8 to 9 minutes. Season the leek mixture lightly with salt and pepper. Remove from the heat.

GREEN BEAN CASSEROLE

3 pounds green beans, trimmed, halved crosswise

2 tablespoons (¼ stick) unsalted butter

2 tablespoons extra-virgin olive oil

5 large leeks (about 2½ pounds total), white and pale green parts only, halved lengthwise, thinly sliced crosswise

1 cup thinly sliced shallots (from about 3 large)

To assemble: Position the rack in the center of the oven and preheat to 350°F. Butter a 14 × 10 × 2-inch or 13 × 9 × 2-inch glass or ceramic baking dish. Transfer the green beans to the prepared baking dish. Spoon the cream of mushroom soup over the beans and thoroughly mix in the soup to coat the beans. Sprinkle the leek mixture evenly over the casserole. Bake until heated through, the mixture bubbles around the edges, and the leeks are golden brown, 35 to 40 minutes. Tent with foil if getting too brown. Remove from the oven and serve.

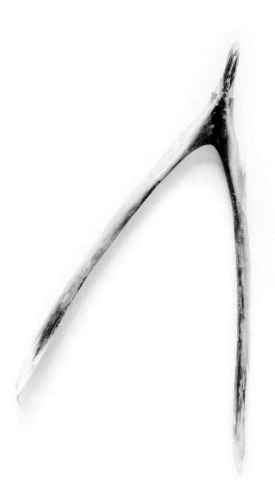

Pumpkin pie with gingersnap cookie crust

SERVES 8 TO 10; BAKE 2 PIES FOR A PARTY

Gingersnaps remind me of my gram. She loves dipping them in her coffee, and a smile always peeks out from her red lips with each bite. Here I use gingersnaps to make a spiced alternative to a regular pie crust. I like using old-school gingersnaps in the crust. You can even bake a sugar pumpkin if you have the time. I'm craving it right now.

CRUST

1½ cups ground gingersnap cookies (25 to 30 cookies)

2 tablespoons sugar

1½ teaspoons ground ginger

¼ teaspoon sea salt

4 tablespoons (½ stick) unsalted butter, melted

FILLING

3 large eggs, beaten to blend

15 ounces cooked sugar pumpkin or organic canned pumpkin

1 cup half and half

¾ cup sugar

1 tablespoon tapioca starch or cornstarch

1 teaspoon vanilla extract

1 teaspoon ground cinnamon

½ teaspoon sea salt

¼ teaspoon ground nutmeg

¼ teaspoon ground cloves

To make the crust: Preheat the oven to 350°F. Combine the ground gingersnap cookies, sugar, ginger, salt, and melted butter in a food processor. Blend until the crumbs are evenly moistened. Press the crumb mixture evenly onto the bottom and up the sides of a 9-inch deep pie dish. Refrigerate the crust for 15 minutes. Bake the crust until set, 12 to 15 minutes. Cool completely. (The crust can be prepared 8 hours ahead. Let stand at room temperature.)

To make the filling: Preheat the oven to 350°F. Whisk the eggs to blend in a medium bowl. Add the remaining filling ingredients, including the pumpkin and whisk until smooth. Pour the filling into the cooled crust. Tap the dish gently on the counter to remove any air bubbles. Bake the pie until the filling is set, 50 to 60 minutes. Transfer the pie to a rack and cool completely.

Cut the pie into wedges and serve with dollops of whipped cream.

Whipped cream: add 2 cups chilled heavy whipping cream, 2 tablespoons vanilla extract, and 1 tablespoon powdered sugar to a stainless steel bowl. Using an electric mixer, beat until peaks form.

december

Tree-trimming cocktail party

If there is ever a month to be a reveler, December is it! I adore the holiday season, and to me that means Christmas music playing from dawn until dusk. This tree-trimming party brings in the yuletide cheer. Keep the mood intimate and festive by using only lights from your tree, the fireplace, and tons of candles. This is a cocktail menu, so sometimes I keep ricotta meatballs simmering in a big pot on the stove or roast a chicken and place it on a cutting board for guests to cut at will. Remember to include in your guest list people who will actually trim the tree instead of spending their night frolicking under the mistletoe.

PARTY OF 16

Eucalyptus Gin Martinis 75

Charcuterie (see page 10)

Pancetta Gougères 76

Endive Spears with Truffle Honey 78

Dark Chocolate Fondue 78

Candy Cane Crunch Cookies 82

Eucalyptus gin martinis

SERVES 2

This recipe came from my friend Elizabeth, who is a real Southern belle. She's the ultimate party guest and is always coming up with inspired concoctions.

EUCALYPTUS SYRUP

2 cups sugar

1 cup water

⅓ cup eucalyptus leaves, chopped or torn in half

MARTINI

1½ cups ice cubes

4 ounces (½ cup) gin

2 ounces (¼ cup) eucalyptus syrup

2 ounces (¼ cup) fresh lime juice

1 egg white

To make the eucalyptus syrup: Combine the sugar and water in a small saucepan. Bring to a boil, stirring until the sugar dissolves. Reduce the heat and simmer for 3 minutes. Add the eucalyptus leaves and simmer for 15 minutes. Remove from the heat; cover and let steep 10 minutes.

Pour the syrup through a strainer into a bowl and cool completely. (The syrup can be prepared 1 month ahead. Store in an airtight container in the refrigerator. Stir before using.)

To make the martini: Combine all the ingredients in a martini shaker and shake vigorously for 30 to 45 seconds. Strain into chilled martini glasses or old-fashioned champagne glasses and serve.

⤳ **Substitute basil for eucalyptus for an equally delicious cockatil.**

Pancetta gougères

MAKES 3 DOZEN

These classic French puffs wow every time. They sound fancy but are really simple to make. They are little bites of heaven.

½ cup dry white wine

½ cup water

8 tablespoons (1 stick) unsalted butter, cubed

1 teaspoon sugar

½ teaspoon kosher salt

1 cup all-purpose flour

4 large eggs

2 cups grated Gruyère

½ cup grated Parmigiano-Reggiano

½ cup pancetta, sautéed and finely chopped

¼ cup chives, finely chopped

Preheat oven to 400°F. Line two baking sheets with parchment paper and set aside.

In a medium saucepan, heat wine, water, butter, sugar, and salt over medium-high heat, until butter is completely melted. Remove from the heat and add cup of flour, stirring vigorously with a wooden spoon until the flour is fully incorporated and the dough pulls away from the sides of the pan, about 2 minutes.

Carefully transfer the dough to a stand mixer. Beat on medium speed for 60 seconds, to cool down. Then beat in the eggs, one at a time. Add grated cheeses, pancetta, and chives. Place rounded tablespoons of dough onto prepared baking sheets, leaving 2 inches between each, as they will expand during baking. Bake for 10 minutes, then reduce oven temperature to 325°F and bake for an additional 15 minutes, until the gougères are golden brown and cooked through to puffy perfection. (The one time we embrace the puffiness!)

It's always a great idea to make these in advance and then pop them into the oven when unexpected guests arrive. Refrigerate dough for up to 3 days or freeze them preformed for 20 minutes, then leave in freezer in plastic bags for up to 3 months. Substitute pancetta with bacon or make them vegetarian. Delish!

Endive spears with truffle honey

A sexy, super simple appetizer that is all about the truffle honey. It's deceivingly simple to make. Lay out the spears, dollop with cheese, and drizzle with honey. The honey is a great hostess gift. You can make it extra decadent with shavings of fresh truffle.

2¼ cups honey

5 to 6 tablespoons truffle oil

4 large heads Belgian endives

6 ounces soft fresh goat cheese, coarsely crumbled

Whisk the honey and 5 tablespoons truffle oil in a medium bowl to blend well. Taste and add 1 more tablespoon truffle oil if desired. Transfer ¼ cup of the truffle honey to a small bowl to reserve for drizzling over the endive spears. Divide the remaining truffle honey among 8 small glass jars to use as gifts.

Cut off the base ends of the endive head and discard. Separate the endive leaves, discarding any bruised leaves. Arrange 32 of the largest endive leaves on a large platter. Sprinkle the crumbled goat cheese onto each leaf, dividing equally. Drizzle ¼ cup truffle honey lightly over the leaves and serve.

Dark chocolate fondue

MAKES 1 POT

A fondue lures everyone in and brings a fun vibe to any gathering. You can serve the fondue with berries, Rice Krispie treats, or kettle chips.

2 cups heavy whipping cream

1 tablespoon instant espresso powder

1½ pounds semisweet chocolate, chopped

1 teaspoon vanilla extract

Three 3-ounce bags of kettle chips with sea salt

Pour the cream and espresso powder in a heavy medium small saucepan and bring to a boil over medium-high heat, stirring until the espresso powder dissolves. Reduce the heat to low. Add the chocolate and whisk over low heat until the mixture is melted and smooth. Stir in the vanilla. Remove from the heat. Pour the chocolate mixture into a fondue pot to keep warm. Serve with kettle chips.

"*The whole world is three drinks behind.*"

—Humphrey Bogart

Candy cane crunch cookies

These cookies are my sister, Kristen's, wintery creation. She is an amazing baker and always makes festive fun cookies that make you feel like a big kid again. From Easy-Bake Ovens to here, I think we are doing okay, sis.

2½ cups all-purpose flour

1 teaspoon sea salt

¾ teaspoon baking soda

16 tablespoons (2 sticks) unsalted butter, softened

1 cup packed golden brown sugar

½ cup sugar

2 teaspoons vanilla extract or vanilla paste

2 large eggs

12 ounces good-quality white chocolate (preferably Lindt because it melts well), coarsely chopped, divided

½ cup coarsely crushed candy canes or peppermint candies

Position the rack in the center of the oven and preheat to 350°F. Line 2 rimmed baking sheets with silicone mats or parchment paper. Whisk the flour, salt, and baking soda in a medium bowl to blend. Beat the butter, both sugars, and vanilla in a large bowl, using an electric mixer. Add eggs and beat the mixture until well blended. Add the flour mixture and beat just until incorporated.

Set aside 2 ounces of the white chocolate for melting and drizzling over the finished cookies. Add the remaining 10 ounces chopped white chocolate to the cookie batter. Form the batter into golf-ball-size balls and place on the prepared baking sheets, spacing 1 to 2 inches apart. Bake the cookies until set and beginning to crack on top, 8 to 10 minutes. Transfer the cookies to a rack and cool completely.

Place the reserved 2 ounces white chocolate in a small metal bowl. Set the bowl over a small saucepan of barely simmering water and stir with a silicone spatula until the chocolate is melted and smooth. Try not to overheat the chocolate or it will seize and will no longer be liquid/ pourable. Remove the bowl from over the water.

Working with 2 to 3 cookies at a time, drizzle the melted white chocolate lightly over the top of the cookies and immediately press some of the crushed candy canes atop each cookie. Repeat the procedure with the remaining cookies, melted chocolate, and crushed candy (it may be necessary to keep the bowl with the melted chocolate over the hot water bath to keep the chocolate melted and warm). Cool the cookies completely. (The cookies can be prepared 3 days ahead. Store in airtight containers in a single layer at room temperature.)

Macadamia nut cookies-follow the cookie recipe but omit the candy canes and the finishing drizzle. Add 1 cup of macadamia nuts, ¾ cup sweetened flaked coconut and you have a perfect year round treat.

New Year's Eve dinner

Time to break out the best of the best and celebrate a year's worth of living. A glamorous hostess serves up an elegant evening inspired by Truman Capote's Black and White Masquerade Ball—allow it to be as wild or composed as you desire. Decadent gruyére fondue and lobster risotto are complimented with winter whites like buttery chardonnays and Perrier-Jouët Belle Epoque Brut Champagne.

PARTY OF 8

Fondue with Roasted Brussels Sprouts 87

Winter Lettuces with Pomegranate Seeds 87

Crab Pots with Lemon Caper Dip 88

Champagne Lobster Risotto 91

Port-Poached Pears 93

Fondue with roasted brussels sprouts

SERVES 8

An old-school classic appetizer to start off a great night.

8 ounces coarsely grated Gruyère cheese

8 ounces coarsely grated Emmentaler Swiss cheese

1½ tablespoons all-purpose flour

1¼ cups dry white wine

1½ teaspoons kirsch

½ teaspoon ground nutmeg

Ground black pepper, to taste

1 garlic clove, peeled and halved

1 pound roasted Brussels sprouts, halved

1 baguette, torn into bite-size pieces

Mix both cheeses with the flour in a medium bowl. Add the wine to a heavy medium saucepan on the stove and bring to a simmer for 3 minutes. Slowly add the cheese mixture to the wine, a handful at a time, stirring in a figure-eight pattern until all the cheese is melted. Stir in the kirsch, nutmeg, and a few grindings of cracked pepper.

Stir constantly over medium-low heat until reduced to desired thickness, about 5 minutes longer. Run the cut sides of the garlic clove all over the inside of the fondue pot. Pour the mixture into a fondue pot and keep warm over canned heat burner. Serve with Brussels sprouts and baguette pieces for dipping.

Winter lettuces with pomegranate seeds

SERVES 8

I love the crimson glow of juicy little pomegranate morsels. Mix with fresh winter lettuces, serve it European style after the entreé, and enjoy.

Shallot vinaigrette (see page 9)

1 pound mix of escarole, endive, radicchio and frisée, torn into bite-size pieces

½ cup fresh pomegranate seeds

Freshly ground pepper to taste

Place the greens in a large bowl. Add the dressing and toss to coat.

Sprinkle the pomegranate seeds over the greens and serve with freshly ground pepper.

Crab pots with lemon caper dip

SERVES 8

The girls in my family recently descended on my house for a weekend recharge. It was filled with Northern California wines and hanging out around the stove. My cousin Zara introduced me to fresh cracked Dungeness crab. Ask your seafood department to order it and have them crack it for you. Lose the heavy bread filling and opt for good ole Hellman's to make these perfect and worthy of a celebration.

LEMON CAPER DIP

½ cup mayonnaise (Hellman's or best foods)

¼ cup fresh lemon juice, or more to taste

Zest of 1 lemon

1 tablespoon capers, finely chopped

CRAB POTS

6 tablespoons mayonnaise

3 tablespoons greek yogurt

1 tablespoon whole grain Dijon mustard

1 small egg, beaten to blend

1 green onion, finely chopped, white and light green parts only

1 teaspoon Worcestershire sauce

1½ teaspoons fresh dill, chopped

Pinch of cayenne pepper

1 pound fresh Dungeness crab

For the dip: Whisk all the ingredients in a small bowl to blend. Season to taste with salt and pepper. (The dip can be made 3 days ahead. Cover and refrigerate.)

For the crab pots: Position the rack in the center of the oven and preheat to 400°F. Spray mini muffin cups with nonstick cooking spray. Whisk the first 8 ingredients in a medium bowl to blend. Gently fold in the crab meat. Fill 24 mini muffin cups with the crabmeat mixture.

Bake for 10 minutes.

Preheat the broiler. Broil the crab pots until a golden brown crust forms on top, 2 minutes. Transfer to plates and serve immediately with the dip alongside.

They are also great as an entrée made in big muffin tins.

Champagne lobster risotto

This divine dish melts in your mouth. Moist nibbles of pink lobster are studded throughout the risotto. Put your guests to work by passing the stirring duties around.

---

4 tablespoons (½ stick) butter, unsalted

¼ cup extra-virgin olive oil

¾ cup chopped white onion

¾ cup chopped green onions, white and pale green parts only

3 garlic cloves, minced

2 cups arborio rice

3 cups Perrier-Jouët Belle Epoque Brut Champagne

3¾ cups lobster stock (I use Better than Bouillon)

1½ cups finely grated Parmesan cheese

4 freshly cooked lobster tails, shelled, cut crosswise into ½-inch chunks

Sea salt and freshly ground black pepper, to taste

3 tablespoons chopped fresh Italian parsley

Melt the butter with the olive oil in a heavy large saucepan over medium-high heat. Add all the onions, and sauté until slightly softened, 2 to 3 minutes. Add the garlic and stir 1 minute. Add the rice and continue to stir 2 minutes. Add the Champagne and bring to a boil. Reduce the heat and simmer 3 minutes, stirring constantly. Add the lobster stock and bring to a boil. Reduce the heat to medium-low and simmer until the rice is tender, stirring frequently, about 25 minutes. Reduce the heat to low. Add the Parmesan and lobster and stir until the risotto is thickened to desired consistency, but still moist and creamy, 3 to 5 minutes longer. Season to taste with salt and pepper. Transfer the risotto to plates. Sprinkle with parsley, and serve.

Make a homemade lobster stock by boiling whole lobster shells with onions, celery, carrots, and fennel if you have the time!

Port-poached pears

SERVES 8

This dish is such a beauty to behold and so easy to prepare. Forgo the long hours baking in the kitchen and enjoy ringing in the new year.

---

4 firm but ripe Bosc pears

One 750-ml bottle port wine

1 cup water

1 cup sugar

1 cinnamon stick

4 whole star anise

One 2-inch-long piece orange peel (orange part only)

One 8-ounce container mascarpone cheese (Italian cream cheese)

Peel the pears in long strokes, creating a smooth outer surface. Cut the pears in half lengthwise and, using a spoon, scoop out the core, creating a hollow for the filling.

Combine the port and water in a large pot and bring to a boil. Add the sugar, cinnamon stick, star anise, and orange peel and lower to a simmer. Add the pear halves and simmer until tender when pierced with a wooden skewer, turning occasionally for even cooking, 15 to 30 minutes, depending on the ripeness of pears. Using a slotted spoon, transfer the pears to a platter to cool.

Remove the cinnamon stick, star anise, and orange peel from the cooking liquid and discard. Continue to simmer the liquid until the port reduction is thick and syrupy, stirring often, 30 to 45 minutes. Cool the syrup. (The pears and syrup can be prepared a day ahead. Cover the pears and syrup separately and refrigerate.)

Fill the hollow in each pear half with a dollop of mascarpone. Place 1 pear half on each plate. Drizzle the port syrup over each half and serve.

january

Detox

January is cleanse month! The stretch of hedonist behavior between Thanksgiving and Christmas makes me want to green my body! The reveler may indulge, but then we have to recharge, too. Replenish your body with vitamin-packed juices, organic soups, and salads. Try to find time to exercise. I can get overwhelmed by all the demands and decisions in life but hiking helps to calm my mind. Detoxing is about feeding your body and soul, taking care of yourself, and honoring your needs. To take care of others you must remember to take care of yourself.

Juices 98

Almond Milk with Dates 99

Arugula with Beets and Blood Oranges 101

Carrot Ginger Soup 102

Almond Meal Cookies 104

Juices

From the vibrant beet juice to the hydrating pineapple and nutrient rich green juice, your body will thank you. Juice away! Each makes about 4 cups.

Beet and carrot juice

1 large red beet with green top, rinsed, chopped

15 carrots, rinsed, chopped

Green juice with lemon

1 large cucumber, rinsed

6 celery stalks, rinsed

4 cups (packed) spinach leaves, kale and/or romaine lettuce, rinsed

One 1-inch piece fresh ginger, peeled, rinsed

1 green apple (such as Granny Smith), rinsed, chopped (optional)

Juice from ½ lemon (about 2 to 3 tablespoons)

Pineapple, cucumber, coconut water, and mint

½ pineapple, skin removed, chopped

1 medium cucumber, unpeeled, rinsed, chopped

½ cup coconut water

5 large fresh mint sprigs

Almond milk with dates

MAKES 2½ CUPS

Homemade almond milk is a creamy delight. You can't even compare it to the store-bought kind. And it's not that hard to make, so give it a shot.

1 cup whole almonds

2½ cups water, or more depending on desired thickness

3 dates, pitted, chopped

Pinch of sea salt

Cheesecloth

To blanch the almonds, place them in a bowl. Add enough water to cover the almonds. Cover the bowl and let the almonds soak at room temperature for 24 to 48 hours.

Drain and rinse the almonds. Combine the almonds, water, dates, and salt in a blender. Blend until frothy. Line a sieve with cheesecloth and set over a bowl. Slowly pour the almond milk through the cheese cloth–lined sieve. Squeeze the cheesecloth to extract as much liquid as possible. Reserve the leftover almond meal in the cheesecloth for cookies! Cover and refrigerate the almond milk.

Arugula with beets and blood oranges

SERVES 2

This is an incredible entrée salad packed with vitamins and nutrients.
You will crave this.

VINAIGRETTE

5 tablespoons hazelnut oil

1 tablespoon fresh blood orange juice

2 teaspoons fresh lemon juice

1 teaspoon minced shallot

½ teaspoon sea salt

½ teaspoon freshly ground black pepper

SALAD

Two 2- to 2½-inch red beets, washed, dried, and trimmed

Two 2- to 2½-inch yellow beets, washed, dried, and trimmed

3 blood oranges, tangelos, mandarins or whatever is fresh.

One 5-ounce package arugula

1 fresh fennel bulb, trimmed, sliced paper-thin

¼ cup hazelnuts, toasted, husked, finely chopped

To make the vinaigrette: Whisk all the vinaigrette ingredients in a small bowl to blend.

To make the salad: Position the rack in the center of the oven and preheat to 400°F. Wrap each beet individually in aluminum foil, enclosing completely. Place on a rimmed baking sheet and bake until the beets are tender when pierced with a wooden skewer or fork, 45 minutes to 1 hour. Remove the beets from the oven and let them stand wrapped in the foil until cool enough to handle. Unwrap the beets and gently rub off the skin (it will slip off easily); discard the skin. Cut the beets crosswise into ⅛-inch-thick rounds. Set aside.

Cut off all the peel and white pith from the oranges. Using a small sharp knife, cut between the membranes to take out the orange segments. Set aside.

Arrange the arugula on a serving platter. Place the beets and orange segments decoratively atop the arugula. Scatter the fennel and hazelnuts over the salad, drizzle with vinaigrette, and serve.

Carrot ginger soup

This bright soup is super healthy with a flavorful kick. The addition of orange juice intensifies the flavor.

2 tablespoons extra-virgin olive oil

½ cup chopped white onion

4 cups chopped carrots

4 cups vegetable broth

1 cup orange juice

1 tablespoon plus 2 teaspoons finely grated fresh peeled ginger

1 tablespoon lemon juice

14-ounce can coconut milk

Freshly ground black pepper, to taste

Heat the olive oil in a large saucepan over medium-high heat. Add the onion and sauté until translucent, about 5 minutes. Add the carrots, broth, orange juice, ginger, and lemon juice; bring to a boil. Reduce the heat and simmer, covered, until the carrots are tender, about 20 minutes. Remove from the heat. Puree with immersion blender or food processor, until very smooth. Return the soup to the saucepan and stir in the coconut milk, salt, and pepper. Reheat the soup over medium heat until hot. Ladle the soup into bowls and serve.

We are so over-sauced, -oiled, -vinegared, and -cheesed. Lightly steam some veggies, with just a touch of sea salt to remember how delicious they can be.

Almond meal cookies

MAKES 3 DOZEN COOKIES

I love making these cookies for my family because they are so healthy. To be honest, sometimes these are the only way I can get myself through a cleanse.

1½ cups ripe mashed bananas (from 4 bananas)

¼ cup coconut oil, warmed

½ teaspoon vanilla extract

½ teaspoon coconut extract

1¾ cups old-fashioned oats

1 cup almond meal (almond milk recipe, page 99)

⅓ cup finely shredded un-sweetened coconut

1 teaspoon baking powder

½ teaspoon ground cinnamon

½ teaspoon sea salt

6 ounces vegan carob chips

Position the rack in the center of the oven and preheat to 350°F. Line 2 rimmed baking sheets with parchment paper or a silicone baking mat. Mix the bananas, coconut oil, vanilla, and coconut extract in a large bowl. Combine the oats, almond meal, shredded coconut, baking powder, cinnamon, and salt in a medium bowl; toss to blend. Add the dry ingredients to the banana mixture and stir until incorporated. Stir in the carob chips. The dough will be moist.

Scoop the dough out by tablespoonfuls and roll into balls. Place on the prepared baking sheets (the cookies will not spread as they bake). Press each dough ball to a ½ inch thickness. Bake until golden, 20 to 22 minutes. Transfer the cookies to a rack and enjoy. Cook in 2 batches.

If using store-bought almond meal, add 2 tablespoons almond milk to compensate for the moistness of homemade almond meal.

Wanderlust supper

When I worked in India, we shot from Mumbai up to the blue city of Jodhpur. The colors and smells made an indelible mark on my life. When I can't get away to travel, I let food be my guide. This exotic vegetarian menu has all the flavors from Morocco to India. Let it transport you.

PARTY OF 6

Chai Tea Latte 108

Warm Spiced Olives 108

Carrots with Savory Yogurt 110

Moroccan Tagine with Preserved Lemons and Couscous 112

Vegan Chocolate Truffles 115

Chai tea latte

SERVES 6

The whole house succumbs to the aroma when making this tea. On ice, it gets me through a mid-afternoon lull.

6 cardamom pods, crushed

1 teaspoon whole cloves

½ teaspoon whole black peppercorns

6 cinnamon sticks

6 cups water

One 3-inch piece fresh ginger, peeled and sliced

1 teaspoon vanilla extract

6 Darjeeling tea bags

3 cups milk, of choice

6 tablespoons agave syrup

Smash the first 3 ingredients in a heavy large saucepan, then add cinnamon sticks. Cook over medium-high heat until fragrant and lightly toasted, about 1 minute. Add 6 cups water, ginger, and vanilla; bring to a boil. Reduce heat and simmer for 10 minutes, uncovered. Add the tea bags, milk, and agave and steep for 10 minutes longer.

Strain the tea into 6 mugs. Place 1 cinnamon stick from the simmered tea in each mug and serve.

Warm spiced olives

SERVES 6

Warm olives drenched in oil and spiced to perfection really does it for me.

1½ cups assorted brine-cured olives

3 sprigs fresh thyme

Two 3-inch orange peel strips

1 tablespoon extra-virgin olive oil

1 bay leaf

1 garlic clove, quartered

1 dried chile (optional)

Combine the first 6 ingredients in a small saucepan. Add the chile, if desired. Cook over medium-low heat until the olives are heated through, stirring occasionally, about 5 minutes. Transfer the olives to a small bowl and serve warm. (See page 106.)

Carrots with savory yogurt

SERVES 6

This homemade yogurt dip is creamy with a kick. The carrots are cooked quickly over high heat, just enough to get a bit of char, but still firm enough to dip. A beautiful appetizer.

YOGURT DIP

1 cup nonfat plain greek yogurt

¼ cup chopped fresh mint

¼ cup extra-virgin olive oil

1½ teaspoons fresh lime juice

½ teaspoon ground cumin

½ teaspoon sea salt

½ teaspoon freshly ground
     black pepper

CARROTS

1 pound multicolored or
     orange carrots sliced in
     half, lengthwise if large

2 tablespoons extra-virgin olive
     oil

To make the dip: Combine all the ingredients for the dip in a small bowl. Whisk to blend.

To make the carrots: Coat the carrots with 2 tablespoons olive oil. Heat a heavy large skillet over high heat. Add the carrots and cook until crisp-tender and slightly charred around the edges, stirring frequently, 4 to 5 minutes (carrots should remain slightly firm for dipping). Cool the carrots completely.

Serve the carrots with the yogurt dip.

Moroccan tagine with preserved lemons and couscous

SERVES 6

This stunning dish is not only vegetarian but vegan. There is no skimping on flavor. Serve in a tagine and you'll feel transported to a different time and place.

2½ cups chopped onions (from about 2 medium), divided

4 tablespoons extra-virgin olive oil, divided

5 garlic cloves, minced

2½ teaspoons paprika

2 teaspoons ground coriander

2 teaspoons ground cumin

1 teaspoon turmeric

1 teaspoon kosher salt

½ teaspoon freshly ground black pepper

½ teaspoon ground ginger

¼ teaspoon cayenne pepper

¼ teaspoon ground cinnamon

1 pound 1-inch peeled cubed butternut squash (about 4 to 4½ cups)

One 1-pound eggplant, unpeeled, cut into 1-inch cubes (about 5 to 6 cups)

Two 15-ounce cans chickpeas, drained and rinsed

One 14½-ounce can chopped tomatoes in juice

Combine ½ cup onions, 2 tablespoons olive oil, garlic, and all the spices in a food processor. Blend until a paste forms, occasionally scraping down the sides of the bowl (the mixture will not be completely smooth). Transfer the spice paste to a small bowl.

Heat the remaining 2 tablespoons oil in a heavy large deep skillet or pot over medium-high heat. Add the remaining 2 cups onions and sauté until the onions begin to soften and turn lightly golden, about 5 minutes. Add the squash and eggplant and sauté 5 minutes. Add the spice paste and stir to coat the vegetables evenly. Continue to sauté until the mixture is fragrant, about 2 minutes. Stir in the chickpeas, tomatoes, broth, lemon juice, and preserved lemon and bring to a boil. Reduce the heat to medium; cover and simmer until the squash and eggplant are very tender and flavors blend, adjusting the heat to medium-low as needed to maintain a simmer, 20 to 25 minutes. Remove from the heat, adjust the seasonings with more salt and pepper, if desired. Stir in the spinach, allow to wilt slightly. Sprinkle with mint (or cilantro) and toasted almonds and serve, passing additional preserved lemons alongside.

One 14½-ounce can vegetable broth

2 tablespoons fresh lemon juice

2 tablespoons preserved lemons, chopped

4 cups baby spinach leaves

½ cup chopped fresh mint or cilantro

½ cup toasted slivered almonds

Preserved Lemons

MAKES ABOUT ¾ CUP

2 large lemons, thinly sliced into rounds, seeds removed

¾ cup water

⅓ cup fresh lemon juice

2 tablespoons extra-virgin olive oil

3½ teaspoons sea salt

Combine all the ingredients in a small skillet. Bring to a boil over medium-high heat, stirring to dissolve the salt. Reduce the heat to medium-low, cover, and simmer until the peel of the lemon slices is very soft, stirring occasionally, 18 to 20 minutes. Remove from the heat.

Cool completely and store in a glass or ceramic jar with a lid. This can be prepared 2 weeks ahead. Cover and refrigerate.

Apricot Couscous

SERVES 4 TO 6

2 cups water

4 ounces dried apricots

1 tablespoon extra-virgin olive oil

1 teaspoon sea salt

One 10-ounce package quick-cooking couscous

½ cup slivered almonds, toasted

Combine water, apricots, olive oil, and salt in a medium saucepan. Bring to a boil. Add the couscous. Remove the saucepan from the heat; cover and let stand until the water is absorbed, about 5 minutes. Add the almonds to the couscous and fluff with a fork to lighten. Divide the couscous among plates and serve.

Vegan chocolate truffles

MAKES 2 DOZEN

You would never believe that these are raw vegan truffles because they are so heavenly and rich. Skip the butter and satiate your chocolate cravings.

1 cup almonds

½ cup raw cacao powder

2 tablespoons plus extra raw coconut butter

¼ cup agave nectar or 6 pitted dates

Pinch sea salt

¼ teaspoon cardamom

½ teaspoon pure vanilla extract

Place almonds in the bowl of a food processor. Pulse until coarsely chopped. Add remaining ingredients and pulse until mixed thoroughly.

Shape mixture into one-inch balls and place in a single layer in a shallow container. Freeze for 30 minutes or until firm.

Keep refrigerated for up to 2 weeks (they'll never last that long!) or freeze in an airtight container or freezer bag for up to a month.

Before freezing, roll truffles in shredded coconut, crushed nuts, goji berries or cacao powder (basically anything yummy). Pig out!

february

Sweethearts soirée

Valentine's Day is a bust, even when you're in love. So skip the cliché dinner; it's so stifled and contrived. Throw a Valentine's Day bash for everyone, couples and singles. I make mine extra easy by setting up a gourmet pizza station. Use premade dough and have your guests choose their favorite toppings. Don't forget a piñata full of grown-up goodies to beat up for those with a broken heart.

PARTY OF 10

Charcuterie (see page 10)

Caesar Salad with Homemade Croutons 120

Artisan Pizzas 121

German Chocolate Cupcakes (see recipe, page 21)

Caesar salad with homemade croutons

My husband loves Caesar salad but hates anchovies. I love flavor, so I created a tart and zesty Caesar that is a staple in our house. I serve it with my meatballs, next to grilled steaks, or with barbecue chicken on top. Make croutons from day-old bread tossed with olive oil, salt, and a dash of garlic powder.

2 large egg yolks

4 teaspoons Dijon mustard

4 cloves garlic, peeled and pressed

1 teaspoon hot sauce

2 teaspoons Worcestershire sauce

1 cup extra-virgin olive oil

1 cup grated Parmesan cheese, plus more for garnish

Juice from 1 lemon

Flaked salt and coarsely ground black pepper, to taste

2 heads romaine lettuce (or 6 romaine hearts), chopped or left in spears and chilled

4 cups croutons

In a large bowl whisk together egg yolk, mustard, garlic, hot sauce, and Worcestershire sauce. While whisking constantly, slowly pour in olive oil. Keep whisking until creamy and smooth.

In a large serving bowl stir in Parmesan cheese and lemon juice. Be sure to taste and add salt and pepper if desired. Top with chopped romaine but do not mix. Chill until ready to serve.

When ready to serve add additional Parmesan cheese, black pepper, and croutons, tossing to coat. Serve immediately.

Artisan pizzas

SERVES 10

Get in the kitchen with all the ones you love and make your own personal pies. My favorite is sausage and broccoli rabe, but don't shy away from trying some more creative toppings, like figs and brie.

PIZZA SAUCE

Three 28-ounce cans plum tomatoes in juice

4½ tablespoons extra-virgin olive oil

1 tablespoon dried oregano

6 garlic cloves, peeled and pressed

3 teaspoons sea salt, or more to taste

2 teaspoons freshly ground black pepper

PIZZA AND TOPPINGS

10 portions of store-bought pizza dough or premade crusts

2½ pounds coarsely grated mozzarella cheese

To make the sauce: Place the tomatoes and their juices in a large bowl. Using a knife and fork, cut up the tomatoes into smaller pieces but still slightly chunky. Add the olive oil, oregano, garlic, salt, and pepper and mix thoroughly. Serve back in the original can.

To make the pizzas and toppings: Preheat the oven to 450°F. If using pizza dough, roll out the dough for each pizza to desired thickness. Allow each guest to spread the sauce atop the dough round or prepared crust and scatter the desired toppings over the sauce. Place the pizzas on baking sheets and bake them until the cheese melts and the crust is golden brown, 12 to 20 minutes, depending on what kind of crust is used. Transfer to plates and serve. (See pages 122–123.)

My favorite toppings: Goat cheese, asiago cheese, sliced prosciutto, crumbled Italian sausage, oil-cured black olives, fresh basil leaves, fresh arugula, thinly sliced red onion, wild mushrooms, broccoli rabe

Super bowl party

If I had it my way, the Philadelphia Eagles would be in the Super Bowl every year. But that's not always the case. Still, the Super Bowl is a great excuse for a party, and the true reveler makes football fare that pleases both fans and foodies. I threw this party for my dad. He had a house full of girls and I watched countless Eagles games with him. No matter the outcome, I always cherished the time together so this day is for you, Dad. Fly, Eagles, fly.

PARTY OF 8

Bloody Mary Bar 126

Goat Cheese–Stuffed Jalapeños 126

Good Girl Gone Bad Cookie Shakes 127

Stilton Dip with Crisp Celery 128

Chicken Cheesesteaks with Caramelized Onions and Fennel 131

Bloody mary bar

This is a build-your-own bar that inspires your friends to get in the game.

Tomato juice

Vodka

Celery stalks with leaves

Lemons

Hot sauce

Green olives stuffed with bleu
    cheese

Celery salt

Worcestershire sauce

Prepared horseradish

Sea salt

Freshly ground black pepper

Chilled cooked shrimp

Allow your guests to create their own concoction, as spicy or salty as they wish.

Goat cheese–stuffed jalapeños

SERVES 8

These are spicy bites of deliciousness. Leave the stem on for a rustic look.

⅔ cup soft fresh goat cheese
    (from one 5-ounce log)

3 tablespoons finely chopped
    red bell pepper

8 jalapeños with stems

8 bacon slices, cut lengthwise

Preheat the oven to 375°F. Mix the goat cheese and the bell pepper in a small bowl. Cut the jalapeños in half lengthwise. Scrape out the seeds and the veins from the jalapeños and discard. Stuff each half with the goat cheese mixture, dividing equally. Wrap each jalapeño half in a half bacon slice and place on a rimmed baking sheet, cheese side up. Bake until the bacon is crisp and the jalapeños are heated through, 10 to 15 minutes. Serve warm. (see page 129)

Good girl gone bad cookie shakes

SERVES 8

These milk shakes are made with Girl Scout cookies. Add some rum and drown your sorrows if your team loses.

1½ cups packed vanilla ice cream

4 cups whole milk

4½ cups crumbled thin mint cookies

1 cup dark rum

4 cups ice cubes

Working in 2 batches, place half the ice cream, milk, cookies, rum, and ice cubes in a blender. Cover and blend until the mixture is smooth. Pour into glasses. Repeat the procedure with the remaining ice cream, milk, cookies, rum, and ice cubes. Serve immediately.

Stilton dip with crisp celery

SERVES 8 TO 10

This is my gourmet cheese twist on a classic buffalo wing dip. Serve with crisp celery sticks and watch people's eyes float from the TV as soon as you put it out.

12 ounces cream cheese, broken into 1-inch chunks, room temperature

6 ounces Stilton cheese or other bleu cheese, coarsely crumbled, room temperature

2½ tablespoons plus 2 teaspoons all-purpose flour, divided

1 cup packed coarsely grated sharp cheddar cheese (about 4 ounces)

¼ cup hot sauce

¼ cup 2-percent milk

¼ cup chopped green onions, white and green parts

Celery sticks for dipping

Combine the cream cheese and the Stilton cheese in a medium bowl. Sprinkle 2½ tablespoons flour over the cheese and toss lightly to coat. Toss the cheddar cheese with the remaining 2 teaspoons flour to coat in a small bowl.

Preheat the broiler. Combine the hot sauce and the milk in a heavy medium saucepan; bring to a simmer over medium-high heat. Add the cream cheese–bleu cheese mixture and stir until the mixture is melted and smooth. Remove from the heat. Pour the melted cheese mixture into a broiler-proof 1-quart baking dish. Sprinkle lightly with freshly ground black pepper and half of the green onions. Sprinkle the cheddar cheese mixture evenly over the cream cheese–bleu cheese mixture, covering the melted cheese in the baking dish completely.

Place the dish under the broiler, about 6 inches from the heat source, and broil just until the cheddar cheese is melted and starts to brown in spots, watching closely to avoid burning, 2 to 3 minutes. Remove from the broiler. Sprinkle the dip with the remaining green onions. Serve immediately with celery sticks for dipping.

Chicken cheesesteaks with caramelized onion and fennel

SERVES 8

Oh, how I miss Philly's own Pat's Steaks with Cheez Whiz. I ended many a night there with friends, scoffing one down in the front seat of a Camaro IROC. This is nothing like it! Here's a grown-up version using chicken with carmelized fennel and shredded fontina. Serve with Dijon mustard, pepperoncini, and hot sauce.

2½ tablespoons butter

3½ tablespoons extra-virgin olive oil, divided

2½ cups white onions, very thinly sliced

1½ teaspoons golden brown sugar

2 teaspoons kosher salt, divided

2 teaspoons freshly ground black pepper

1½ cups fresh fennel bulb, thinly sliced

3 baguettes, cut crosswise into eight 6-inch-long pieces total, each piece cut in half horizontally

2½ pounds boneless skinless chicken breasts, cut into 2 inch slices

1¾ pounds Fontina cheese, coarsely grated

Melt the butter with 2½ tablespoons oil in a heavy large skillet (preferably cast-iron) over medium heat. Add the onion and sauté 5 minutes. Add the brown sugar, half the salt, and pepper; reduce the heat to medium-low and sauté 10 minutes. Add the fennel and continue to sauté until the vegetables are deep golden brown and caramelized, stirring occasionally and scraping up any browned bits, 20 to 30 minutes longer. Transfer to a covered bowl.

In the same pan heat 1 tablespoon oil over medium heat. Saute chicken breasts with remaining salt and pepper 3–4 minutes per side or until cooked through. Stir in reserved fennel and onion mixture. Remove from heat.

Preheat the broiler. Scoop the chicken and vegetables onto the bottom halves of the baguette slices and top with cheese. Broil the sandwiches, open-faced, until the cheese melts and the bread is warm, 2 to 4 minutes. Remove from the oven. Transfer to plates and serve.

march

Movie night meals

Some nights are meant for collapsing on the couch and tuning out. I treasure these nights—they are meant for watching movies. These dishes are for those evenings because they don't require a lot of preparation and most can be made using only one pan. So be like Bogart and just chill.

PARTY OF 2 TO 4

Tlalpeno soup   136

Sizzling Brown Rice Bowls   137

Eggplant Towers with Ground Lamb and Yogurt Sauce   138

Steak au Poivre   141

Nutella Macaroons   142

Tlalpeno soup

I discovered this soup while I was in Mexico. A couple of years ago, I was down there shooting a movie, and midway through production, I went down for the count with the flu. I just wanted some chicken noodle soup. One of the local crewmembers brought me Tlalpeno soup. It was a godsend; the chipolte peppers cleared my congestion and the bay leaf-infused chicken broth helped put me back on my feet. It really warms you up.

---

4 quarts (16 cups) water

One 4-pound whole chicken with skin and bones intact (preferably organic)

1 medium white onion, thickly sliced

4 celery stalks, quartered

2 carrots, peeled, quartered

5 bay leaves

1 tablespoon whole black peppercorns

3 teaspoons sea salt

Juice from 3 limes (about ⅓ cup)

¼ cup chipotle chile peppers in adobo sauce, pureed in a food processor until smooth

1 tablespoon bouillon chicken base or bouillon cubes

4 cups cooked white or brown rice

Freshly ground black pepper

1 avocado, peeled, pitted, sliced

Chopped fresh cilantro, for garnish

Bring 4 quarts of water to a boil in an 8-quart pot over high heat. Add the chicken, onion, celery, carrots, bay laves, and peppercorns and bring to a boil. Reduce the heat to medium-low and simmer, slightly covered, for 1 hour.

Remove the chicken from the cooking liquid; place on a platter and let stand at room temperature until cool. Shred the meat from the chicken; discard the skin and bones.

Pour the cooking liquid from the 8-quart pot into a strainer set over a large bowl. Discard the solids in the strainer. Add enough of the strained cooking liquid to the pot with the shredded chicken to cover by 2 inches (reserve any remaining cooking liquid for another use). Stir in the lime juice, pureed chipotles, and bouillon. Bring to simmer over medium heat. Simmer for 10 minutes. Stir in the rice. Remove from the heat. Ladle the soup into 4 serving bowls. Sprinkle lightly with freshly ground black pepper. Garnish each serving with avocado slices and cilantro, serve.

Sizzling brown rice bowls

SERVES 2

This dish has barely any oil, but still has a wonderful gingery glaze.

¼ cup rice wine vinegar

2 teaspoons packed brown sugar

2 teaspoons Sriracha

2 tablespoons sherry or dry white wine

4 teaspoons tamari soy sauce, divided

3 teaspoons extra-virgin olive oil, divided

2 teaspoons toasted sesame oil, divided

2 cups cooked brown rice, cooled

1 teaspoon plus 1 tablespoon grated peeled fresh ginger, divided

8 ounces boneless, skinless chicken thighs, cut in 2 x ½-inch pieces

3½ ounces fresh shiitake mushrooms, stemmed and cut into ½-inch wide strips

4 green onions, sliced, white and green parts, divided

2 garlic cloves, peeled and minced

6 ounces baby bok choy, washed and trimmed

Toasted sesame seeds

In a small bowl, stir the first four ingredients plus 2 teaspoons soy sauce to blend.

Heat 2 teaspoons of the olive oil and 1 teaspoon sesame oil in a wok or heavy, large nonstick skillet over medium-high heat. Add the rice, 1 teaspoon ginger, and 2 teaspoons soy sauce and stir-fry until the rice is golden brown and heated through, about 4 minutes. Divide the rice between two bowls. (Keep the rice warm.)

Return the wok to medium-high heat (no need to wash). Add the remaining 1 teaspoon olive oil and 1 teaspoon sesame oil and heat until the skillet is very hot, about 1 minute. Add the chicken, mushrooms, white parts of the green onions, garlic, and the remaining 1 tablespoon ginger and stir-fry until the chicken is just cooked through and the mushrooms are just tender, about 4 minutes. Scatter the bok choy over the chicken and mushrooms and spoon the sherry mixture over. Stir-fry until the bok choy is tender and the chicken and mushrooms are glazed, about 2 minutes. Top the rice with the chicken and vegetables, dividing equally. Sprinkle the rice bowls with the sliced green onion tops and sesame seeds. Drizzle Sriracha over, if desired, and serve.

Eggplant towers with ground lamb and yogurt sauce

SERVES 4

This recipe is a satisfying creamy dish with Middle Eastern flavors that meld together deliciously. Serve with herbed quinoa.

Two 12- to 16-ounce eggplants, unpeeled, trimmed, cut crosswise into twelve ⅓-inch thick rounds

Extra-virgin olive oil

1 teaspoon kosher salt, divided

1 teaspoon freshly ground black pepper, divided

½ cup minced white onion

1 large garlic clove, peeled and minced

2 teaspoons ground cumin

½ teaspoon ground cinnamon

1 pound ground lamb

¼ cup dry vermouth

1 cup plain low-fat Greek yogurt

5 ounces soft fresh goat cheese, coarsely crumbled

4 cups spinach leaves (about half of a 5-ounce package baby spinach leaves)

Position the oven rack in the center of the oven and preheat to 350°F. Rub the eggplant slices generously on both sides with olive oil. Arrange the eggplant slices in single layers on 2 rimmed baking sheets, spacing apart. Sprinkle the eggplant slices with ½ teaspoon salt and ½ teaspoon freshly ground pepper. Roast in the oven until the eggplant slices begin to soften, about 10 minutes. Turn the slices over and bake them 5 minutes longer. Remove from the oven and set aside the eggplant slices still on the baking sheets. Maintain the oven temperature.

Heat 1 tablespoon olive oil in a heavy large skillet over medium-high heat. Add the onion and sauté until tender and golden, about 5 minutes. Add the garlic, then cumin and cinnamon; stir 30 seconds. Add the ground lamb, remaining ½ teaspoon salt, and ½ teaspoon pepper to the skillet and sauté until the meat is cooked through, breaking up into small pieces with a wooden spoon, about 8 minutes.

Add the vermouth to the skillet and cook until almost evaporated, about 1 minute. Add the yogurt, then the goat cheese; stir until well blended. Reduce the heat to low, cover, and simmer until the mixture is creamy, stirring occasionally, 3 to 5 minutes. Remove the skillet from the heat.

Place 4 of the larger eggplant slices, side by side, in a single layer in the bottom of an 8x8-inch glass or ceramic baking dish. Top each eggplant slice with a generous layer of spinach, then divide ⅓ of the lamb mixture among the slices. Repeat, layering the eggplant slices, spinach, and lamb one more time, forming a stack. Top the stacks with the remaining 4 eggplant slices, then the remaining lamb mixture, dividing equally. Tent the baking dish with aluminum foil and bake in the oven at 350°F until the eggplant stacks are tender and heated through, about 30 minutes. Serve.

Steak au poivre

SERVES 2

This is a classic French dish; the sauce pairs perfectly with filet mignon, but you can use any steak you like. I fell for steak au poivre at Raoul's in New York City, and my love for it has never wavered. It's rich, fabulous, sexy, and decadent.

2 tablespoons crushed black peppercorns

1 teaspoon fennel seeds

½ teaspoon kosher salt

Two 6- to 8-ounce filet mignons (beef tenderloin), about 1 inch thick

3 teaspoons extra-virgin olive oil, divided

3½ teaspoons unsalted butter, divided

1 tablespoon minced shallot (from 1 small)

¼ cup Cognac or brandy

¾ cup beef stock or beef broth

2½ tablespoons heavy whipping cream

Chopped fresh parsley, for garnish

Crush the peppercorns and fennel seeds in a mortar and pestle. Add salt. Coat the filet mignon on both sides with the peppercorn mixture.

Melt 2 teaspoons olive oil with 2 teaspoons butter in a heavy skillet (preferably cast-iron) over medium-high heat. Add the filet mignon to the skillet and cook to desired doneness, 2 to 3 minutes per side for medium-rare. Transfer the filets to a plate; tent with foil to keep warm. Remove the skillet from the heat and cool 1 to 2 minutes. (Do not clean the skillet.)

Melt the remaining butter with the oil in the same skillet over medium-high heat. Add the shallot and sauté 1 minute. Add the Cognac and boil to reduce slightly, about 1 minute, scraping up any browned bits from the bottom of the skillet. Add the beef stock and boil until reduced by half, 2 to 3 minutes. Add the cream and boil until thickened to desired consistency, stirring occasionally, 2–3 minutes.

Plate the filet mignon. Pour the sauce over the steak. Garnish with chopped parsley and serve.

Nutella macaroons

These macaroons are a quick, guilt-free pleasure. The espresso bumps up the flavor of the chocolate.

---

2 large egg whites

1 tablespoon instant espresso powder dissolved in 1 tablespoon hot water

1 teaspoon vanilla extract

½ teaspoon sea salt

5 tablespoons Nutella (hazelnut spread)

One 7-ounce package sweetened flaked coconut

Position the oven rack in the center of the oven and preheat to 350°F. Line a large rimmed baking sheet with parchment paper. Vigorously whisk the egg whites in a large bowl. Add espresso mixture, vanilla, and salt and continue blending. Add Nutella and continue to whisk. Add the coconut and mix until thoroughly blended.

Drop the macaroon mixture by tablespoonfuls onto the prepared baking sheet, spacing apart and forming each into a pyramid shape with your fingers.

Bake the macaroons until lightly browned on the outside but still moist on the inside, 12 to 15 minutes. Remove the baking sheet from the oven. Let the cookies stand on the baking sheet for 5 minutes, then transfer to a rack to cool completely. (The macaroons can be prepared 1 day ahead. Store in an airtight container at room temperature.)

"First learn
the rules . . . then
break them."

Slumber party

The vibe is cigar lounge, leather sofas, backgammon, whiskey sours, cheeseburgers, and men's striped pajamas. An evening full of old-school nostalgia. Invite over a bunch of friends to celebrate a birthday, bachelorette, or just a good old hang. Boys do it good but girls do it better.

PARTY OF 4

Whiskey Sours 147

Buttermilk Ranch Wedge 148

Ultimate Whiskey Bacon Cheeseburger 151

Kettle Chip and Crème Fraîche–Baked Onion Rings 152

Decadent Brownies 153

your
beautiful
mystery

Whiskey sours

One summer night, I was sitting in a friend's backyard under an old lemon tree. As the sun set, we grabbed some lemons, sugar, and whiskey, and piled them on the wood table. We played the Allman Brothers and got lost in the night.

¾ cup fresh lemon juice

4 teaspoons superfine sugar

6 cups ice cubes

1½ cups whiskey

4 maraschino cherries

Stir the lemon juice and sugar in a 1-cup measuring cup until the sugar dissolves. Divide the ice cubes among 4 tumbler glasses. Pour 6 tablespoons whiskey and 3 tablespoons of the lemon juice mixture into each glass. Stir to blend. Garnish each with 1 maraschino cherry and serve.

Buttermilk ranch wedge

SERVES 4; MAKES 3 CUPS OF DRESSING

If you're going to do it, do it right. You'll never touch the bottled version again. Homemade, creamy, deliciousness with lots of fresh herbs.

2¼ cups mayonnaise

¾ cup buttermilk, shaken

¼ cup finely chopped fresh Italian parsley

3 tablespoons finely chopped fresh chives

3 tablespoons packed finely chopped fresh dill

2 teaspoons apple cider vinegar

2 teaspoons onion powder

1¼ teaspoons Worcestershire sauce

¼ teaspoon sea salt

½ teaspoon, generous, freshly ground black pepper

1 large garlic clove, peeled and pressed, or 1 teaspoon granulated garlic

1 head iceberg lettuce, outer layer of leaves removed, lettuce head cut into 4 wedges

Combine all the ingredients except the lettuce in a medium bowl. Whisk until well blended. Cover the dressing and refrigerate at least 1 hour to allow the flavors to develop. (The dressing can be prepared 1 week ahead. Keep refrigerated.)

Rinse the lettuce wedges under cold running water; shake off the excess water. Place the wedges in a glass bowl. Cover with a moistened paper towel and refrigerate up to 4 hours. The wet paper towel will add crispness to the lettuce.

Place 1 lettuce wedge on each of 4 plates. Spoon generous amount of ranch dressing over each, crack fresh pepper on top, and serve.

Ultimate whiskey bacon cheeseburger

SERVES 4

Look at the burger. Enough said.

SECRET SAUCE

½ cup mayonnaise

¼ cup ketchup

¼ cup finely chopped dill pickle

¼ cup finely chopped pepper-oncini

BURGERS

8 thick-cut apple-wood smoked bacon slices

1 tablespoon whiskey

8 ounces ground sirloin

8 ounces ground chuck

¼ teaspoon kosher salt

¼ teaspoon freshly ground black pepper

Four ⅓-inch thick slices sharp Cheddar cheese

4 soft white hamburger buns

Butter

To make the secret sauce: Whisk all the sauce ingredients in a small bowl to blend. Cover and refrigerate. (The sauce can be made 3 days ahead. Keep refrigerated.)

To make the burgers: gently mix the ground sirloin, chuck, salt and pepper in a medium bowl. Form the mixture into 4 even patties.

Arrange the bacon slices side by side in a heavy skillet. Pour the whiskey over the bacon. Cook over medium heat until the bacon is browned and crisp. Remove from pan and cover bacon to keep warm. Pour out excess grease.

Add the meat patties to the skillet with the bacon drippings. Cook patties for 2 minutes over medium-high heat (do not press down patties with a spatula). Turn patties over and place 2 bacon slices, then 1 slice cheese atop each patty. Cover the skillet with a lid and cook the patties until the cheese is melted and the meat is cooked to desired doneness, about 2 minutes longer for medium-rare. Meanwhile, butter the hamburger buns and place in a toaster oven just until warmed through but still soft. Top each with a patty. Spoon the secret sauce generously over each patty, cover and serve.

Kettle chip and crème fraîche–baked onion rings

SERVES 4

I just have something against frying. It intimidates me and makes me feel too . . . greasy. These onion rings will rival your favorite dive-bar snack, and I also serve them on top of my pan-seared New York Steak (page 16) with sautéed spinach to complete the meal.

One 5-ounce bag plain salted kettle or other Hawaiian-style potato chips

½ cup crème fraîche

1½ tablespoons milk

¼ teaspoon freshly ground black pepper

⅛ teaspoon cayenne pepper

⅛ teaspoon kosher salt

½ cup all-purpose flour

Twelve ½-inch thick onion rings, each about 2 to 3 inches in diameter

Position the rack in the center of the oven and preheat to 450°F. Place the potato chips in the food processor and process until the chips are ground. Transfer the chips to a medium bowl.

Whisk the crème fraîche, milk, pepper, cayenne, and salt to blend in a deep medium bowl. Place the flour in another medium bowl. Line up the bowls like an assembly line on a workspace and set a heavy large baking sheet next to the bowls. Using a fork, dip one onion ring in the flour mixture, then dunk it in the crème fraîche mixture, and then place rings into chips mixture and scoop the crumbs up over the ring to coat. The chips should cling very well. Transfer the ring to the baking sheet. Repeat the dipping process until all twelve rings are coated with flour, crème fraîche mixture, and chips. Bake until the onion rings are golden brown and the onions are tender when pierced with a knife, about 15 minutes. Cool slightly and serve.

Decadent brownies

MAKES 16 BROWNIES

This book would not be complete without a perfect brownie. A dense, chocolatey bite of sin. Go ahead, indulge.

1 cup unsweetened cocoa powder

¾ cup all purpose flour

1 teaspoon sea salt

3 large eggs

2¾ cups sugar

1 teaspoon vanilla extract

2½ sticks unsalted butter, melted

3.5 ounces dark chocolate, crushed into ¼ chunks

Powdered sugar (for garnish)

Position the oven rack in the center of the oven and preheat to 350°F. Butter a 9 x 9-inch square cake pan, line with oversided parchment, to be used as "handles," and butter parchment. Whisk the cocoa powder, flour, and salt in a medium bowl to blend. Using an electric mixer, beat the eggs in large bowl, add sugar and vanilla and mix until well blended. Add the melted butter and cocoa mixture. Stir in the crushed chocolate.

Transfer the mixture to the prepared baking pan; spread evenly. Bake until a tester inserted into the center of the brownie comes out with a few moist crumbs still attached, 45–50 minutes. Remove from the oven and cool completely. Use butter parchment "handles" to easily remove brownies from pan. Cut into 16 squares. Dust with powdered sugar and serve.

april

Alfresco lunch

Pack away the puffy down coat and lose that extra hour of sleep—spring is here! On the first warm weekend, we love to go for a drive with the dogs on the Pacific Coast Highway to the beach up in Malibu. When you go on road trips you're at the mercy of fast food, so I like to pack a fresh lunch. Romanticize the occasion—whether you're hiking in the mountains, having an afternoon in the park, or going for a drive by the sea. This is a great picnic.

PARTY OF 8

Baby Mac's Organic Granola   159

Spring Sugar Snap Pea Salad with Fresh Mint   160

Ficelle Sandwiches with Roasted Turkey, Brie, and Fig Chutney   163

Macadamia Nut Cookies (see page 83, tip)

Baby mac's organic granola

SERVES 8; MAKES ABOUT 9 CUPS

I concocted this granola when I was pregnant with my son Teddy so that I had a snack when I was hiking, or as a pick-me-up on the go. And now he enjoys it, too—whether he remembers or not, one of the first things he asked for was more "nola." The chia seeds, macadamia nuts, and coconut oil are packed with health and the "good" oils that make your skin glow.

1 cup coconut oil

¾ cup agave syrup

2 teaspoons vanilla extract

2 teaspoons ground cinnamon

1 teaspoon coconut extract

¼ teaspoon kosher salt

3 cups old-fashioned oats

1 cup macadamia nuts, coarsely chopped

1 cup shelled natural pumpkin seeds (pepitas)

½ cup flax seeds

½ cup chia seeds

1½ cups unsweetened shaved coconut

1 cup dried cranberries

Position the rack in the center of the oven and preheat to 350°F. Combine the coconut oil, agave, vanilla, cinnamon, coconut extract, and salt in a bowl; whisk until well blended.

Combine the oats, macadamia nuts, pumpkin seeds, flax seeds, and chia seeds in a large bowl; stir to blend. Pour the coconut oil mixture over the oat mixture and stir to blend thoroughly. Spread the mixture in a thin, even layer on a large rimmed baking sheet. Bake until the mixture begins to turn golden brown, stirring frequently, about 20 minutes. Mix in the shaved coconut and cranberries. Continue to bake until the granola is crisp and deep golden, stirring frequently, 10 to 15 minutes longer. Remove from the oven; stir to loosen the granola from the baking sheet if necessary. Cool completely on the baking sheet. (Can be prepared 1 week ahead. Store in an airtight container at room temperature.)

Spring sugar snap pea salad with fresh mint

SERVES 8

This is spring fresh at its best!

SHALLOT VINAIGRETTE

(see page 9)

SALAD

2 pounds sugar snap peas, strings removed

Ice cubes

½ cup fresh mint leaves, very thinly sliced

Edible flowers (optional)

To make the salad: Fill a large bowl with water and ice cubes and place close to the stove. Steam the snap peas in a steamer set over boiling water just until the peas are crisp-tender but still bright green, 1 to 2 minutes. Immediately plunge the snap peas into the bowl with the ice water for 1 to 2 minutes to stop the cooking. Drain well. Add the snap peas to another bowl with the vinaigrette and toss to coat. Transfer the pea mixture to a serving bowl. Sprinkle the mint over the snap peas. Garnish with edible flowers and a light sprinkling of flaked salt, if desired, and serve.

"*Keep trying, hold on and always always always believe in yourself, because if you don't then who will, sweetie.*"

—Marilyn Monroe

Ficelle sandwiches with roasted turkey, brie, and fig chutney

Turkey is not just for Thanksgiving. Every month or two I roast a breast and snack on it all week. This will be your favorite grab and go sandwich.

One 2½- to 3-pound bone-in turkey breast with skin

4 tablespoons (½ stick) herb butter (see September recipe page 16)

1 cup dry white wine

8 slender mini baguettes or ficelles, each about 6 inches long, halved horizontally

1½ pounds brie cheese, rind removed, room temperature

Fig Chutney (see page 29)

Preheat the oven to 400°F. Place the turkey breast on a rimmed baking sheet. Using your fingers, carefully loosen the skin on the turkey breast with your fingers and spread the herb butter over the breast under the skin. Roast the turkey breast for 10 minutes. Reduce the oven temperature to 350°F. Pour the wine over the turkey and baste with some of the herb butter pan drippings. Continue to roast until an instant-read thermometer inserted into the thickest part of the turkey breast registers 170°F and the juices run clear when the turkey is pierced with a fork, basting frequently with the pan drippings, 45 minutes to 1 hour.

Remove the turkey breast from the oven and let stand for 10 to 15 minutes. Scrape up the crusty bits from the pan and mix them into the pan juices and continue to baste the turkey breast while it cools slightly. Thinly slice the turkey breast.

Spread the brie cheese lightly over both cut sides of the mini baguettes. Layer generously with turkey slices. Top each with a layer of fig chutney.

Add pomegranate juice or grenadine to lemonade for a quick blush drink.

Spring clothing swap

The reveler is thrifty—one gal's trash is another's gal's treasure. Whether you've never worn an item or worn it to too many dinners, here is a party to give your wardrobe an update without having to spend any money. Have your girlfriends bring over three to four pieces of clothing or accessories that they just don't wear anymore. Throw them all on the bed and find a new treasure. Everyone walks away with a bounty! I make the mushroom crostini before everyone arrives and then enlist a girlfriend to make the salad while I sear the scallops. Dinner for all in less than 15 minutes. Quick recipes so you can spend your time hanging out with your friends.

PARTY OF 6

Charcuterie (see page 10)

Mixed Mushrooms on Olive Crostini 167

Mache with Truffle Vinaigrette 168

Scallops with Jalapeño 168

Vegan Chocolate Truffles (see page 115)

Mixed mushrooms on olive crostini

SERVES 6

I run to this dish. Goat cheese topped with herbs and glistening mushrooms. Yum. Try to get a nice variety of mushrooms to make this crostini a stunner.

Six ½-inch thick slices crusty olive bread

3 tablespoons extra-virgin olive oil, divided

2 tablespoons plus 1 teaspoon unsalted butter, divided

1½ pounds assorted fresh wild mushrooms (such as crimini, oyster, porcini, enoki, and shiitake), sliced

2 tablespoons fresh lemon juice (from about ½ lemon)

2 tablespoons chopped fresh thyme

1 tablespoon chopped fresh sage

1 tablespoon chopped fresh parsley

1 tablespoon chopped fresh basil

½ teaspoon (or more) kosher salt

¼ teaspoon (or more) freshly ground black pepper

One 4- to 5-ounce log soft fresh goat cheese

6 fresh thyme sprigs or micro-greens, for garnish (optional)

Toast slices of the olive bread. Brush the bread with 2 tablespoons olive oil. Allow to slightly cool.

Melt 2 tablespoons butter with 1 tablespoon olive oil in a heavy large skillet over medium-high heat. Add the mushrooms, lemon juice, chopped thyme, sage, ½ teaspoon salt, and ¼ teaspoon pepper and sauté until the mushrooms are well-browned and tender but not dry, stirring occasionally, 8 to 10 minutes. Stir in the parsley and basil. Mix in the remaining 1 teaspoon butter. Taste and adjust the seasoning with more salt and pepper, if desired.

Spread the goat cheese evenly over the toasts. Top each with the mushroom mixture, dividing equally. Garnish each with 1 thyme sprig or microgreens and serve.

Mache with truffle vinaigrette

SERVES 6

This is a lovely, light salad. The truffle really adds something special. This salad is also amazing with grilled salmon.

Truffle vinaigrette (see page 36)

5-ounce mache lettuce

1 ripe pear, unpeeled, cored, thinly sliced

¼ teaspoon truffle salt

¼ teaspoon freshly ground black pepper

Place the mache in a medium serving bowl. Add the vinaigrette and toss to coat. Scatter the pear slices over the greens. Sprinkle with the truffle salt and cracked pepper and serve.

Scallops with jalapeño

SERVES 6

This dish packs a wow factor like the beauty that created it. Just like my best friend Tracy it's sexy, fun in a flash, and unpretentious.

SCALLOPS

24 large sea scallops

Kosher salt and freshly ground black pepper, to taste

2 tablespoons extra-virgin olive oil, divided

2 tablespoons (¼ stick) butter

Three sprigs fresh parsley

Three sprigs fresh thyme

Three sprigs fresh tarragon

Sticky rice, cooked

5 fresh jalapeños, sliced

Sprinkle the scallops lightly with salt and pepper. Heat a heavy large skillet (preferably cast-iron) over high heat. Add 1 tablespoon oil to the skillet and heat until almost smoking. Add half of the scallops to the skillet and cook until golden brown on the bottom, 1½ to 2 minutes. Quickly turn the scallops over and brown on the second side, about 30 seconds. Transfer the scallops to a bowl. Repeat with the remaining scallops. Return all the scallops to the hot skillet over high heat, then add the butter and the herb sprigs, swirling the skillet vigorously and spooning the melted butter over the scallops just until they are opaque in the center, about 30 seconds to 1 minute longer. Discard the sprigs.

Spoon the sticky rice onto 6 plates, dividing equally. Place 4 scallops along with the juices from the skillet atop the rice on each serving. Top the scallops with the jalapeño slices and serve immediately.

may

Earth mother's brunch

This is a holiday where I like to include everyone. People who aren't with their moms, the moms, and people who want to be moms. It's for anyone who has a special connection with their family. As a new mother, traditions mean more to me now than ever.

In this menu I share time-tested recipes and the secrets about them. It has lots of fresh green flavors and is light, with decadent twists. This relaxed brunch could be for a bridal or baby shower or even someone's birthday. Entertaining is about getting your friends together and showing them how special they are.

PARTY OF 10

White Peach Bellinis 175

Peppermint and Lemon Verbena Tea 175

Crudités with Arugula Pesto 177

Crostini with Smashed Peas and Pecorino 178

Lump Crab in Lettuce Cups 181

Leek and Asparagus Crustless Quiche 182

Triple Berry Upside Down Cake 185

White peach bellinis

SERVES 10

Bellini . . . There is rarely a day that I wouldn't love to have you! My first bellini was at Cipriani, and it was a glamorous affair. This bellini is perfect to make when peaches are at their ripest, but you can also use gourmet peach juice.

Two 750-ml bottles chilled Perrier-Jouët Grand Brut Champagne

Cheesecloth

5 very ripe white peaches, peeled, halved, pitted, or 1½ cups canned peach nectar

Line a large strainer with a layer of cheesecloth and set the strainer over a large bowl. Place the peaches in a food processor and puree until smooth. Pour the peach puree into the cheesecloth-lined strainer. Using a silicone spatula, press on the peach puree to extract as much juice as possible into the bowl (some of the pulp will be pressed through the cheesecloth). Discard the remaining puree in the cheesecloth.

Spoon 2 to 3 tablespoons peach juice into each of 10 champagne flutes. Fill the flutes with champagne and serve.

Peppermint and lemon verbena tea

SERVES 10

I love mint and I always grow it in my garden. This is inspired by classic Moroccan mint tea. It is a wonderful relaxing end to any meal and is also refreshing over ice.

8 cups water

2 ounces fresh peppermint leaves (about 1 packed cup)

2 ounces fresh lemon verbena leaves (about 1 packed cup)

2 to 4 tablespoons honey

Bring 8 cups water to boil in a kettle or medium saucepan. Place the peppermint leaves and lemon verbena leaves in a large heatproof pitcher. Pour the hot water into the pitcher over the leaves. Add the honey and muddle the leaves with a wooden spoon. Cover and let stand 10 minutes for flavors to develop. Pour the tea into glasses and serve.

Crudités with arugula pesto

SERVES 10

Arugula adds a peppery punch to your traditional pesto. Look for interesting vegetables with beautiful colors, like radishes and heirloom carrots. Arrange piled high on a beautiful serving tray with your homemade pesto drizzled with olive oil. By the way, this pesto is perfect to toss with pasta.

ARUGULA PESTO

1 cup packed fresh arugula

1 cup packed fresh basil leaves

⅓ cup pine nuts

1 large garlic clove, peeled and pressed

1½ teaspoons fresh lemon juice

¼ teaspoon sea salt

¼ teaspoon freshly ground black pepper

¾ cup extra-virgin olive oil

⅔ cup parmesan cheese

CRUDITÉS:

Trimmed asparagus spears

Heirloom carrots

Belgian endive spears

Bell peppers

Celery sticks

Cucumber slices

Grape tomatoes

Green beans

Radishes

Sugar snap peas

To make the pesto: Combine the arugula, basil, pine nuts, garlic, lemon juice, salt, and pepper in a food processor. Puree. Gradually add the olive oil through the feed tube and process until the pesto is almost smooth. Transfer the pesto to a bowl, and mix in parmesan cheese. (The pesto can be prepared 6 hours ahead. Cover and refrigerate. Let stand at room temperature for 1 hour before serving.)

Arrange the crudités decoratively on a serving platter. Place the bowl of pesto alongside, drizzle with extra-virgin olive oil if desired, and serve.

Crostini with smashed peas and pecorino

SERVES 10

This recipe features classic Italian flavors. The saltiness of the pecorino balances the sweetness of the peas. So easy to make, but try not to over-blend because you want texture.

3 cups frozen green peas

¾ cup whole-milk ricotta cheese (about 6 ounces)

3 tablespoons chopped fresh basil

2½ tablespoons fresh lemon juice

2 tablespoons finely grated Pecorino cheese

½ teaspoon sea salt

¼ teaspoon freshly ground black pepper, plus additional for sprinkling

1 sourdough baguette, cut on diagonal into ½-inch-thick slices

Extra-virgin olive oil

Pecorino Romano shavings (cut with a vegetable peeler)

Micro-greens or whole frozen peas, thawed, for garnish (optional)

Cook the peas in a medium saucepan of boiling salted water until just tender, about 2 minutes. Drain well. Transfer peas to a medium bowl. Add to the peas, ricotta cheese, basil, lemon juice, 2 tablespoons grated Pecorino, salt, and pepper. Smash ingredients together with a fork until pea mixture is chunky.

Preheat the oven to 350°F. Arrange the baguette slices in a single layer on a rimmed baking sheet. Drizzle with olive oil and bake just until lightly toasted, about 10 minutes. Remove from the oven and cool the bread on the baking sheet.

Spread the pea puree on the toasted baguette slices, dividing equally. Top with Pecorino shavings. Sprinkle lightly with pepper. Garnish with micro-greens, if desired, and serve.

Lump crab in lettuce cups

SERVES 10

This is crab with a kick. Sambal Oelek is a chili paste made with vinegar that you can find at most markets. It balances the sweetness of the crab. It is spicy, so adjust the amount used to your taste. Zesting is also a way that really enhances the flavors.

½ cup mayonnaise

4½ teaspoons Sambal Oelek chile paste

4 teaspoons fresh lemon juice

2 teaspoons finely grated lemon zest (from about 1½ lemons)

¼ teaspoon sea salt

¼ teaspoon freshly ground black pepper

1 pound fresh lump crabmeat, picked over

1 head of butter lettuce

2 green onions, thinly sliced

2 tablespoons finely chopped fresh chives

Whisk the mayonnaise, chili paste, lemon juice, lemon zest, salt, and pepper in a medium bowl to blend. Gently fold in the crabmeat.

Arrange the butter lettuce leaves on a serving platter. Spoon the crab mixture onto the center of each leaf, dividing equally. Sprinkle lightly with the green onions and chives and serve.

Leek and asparagus crustless quiche

SERVES 10

When I was developing this menu, I wanted to find the right balance of decadence without feeling weighed down. A frittata without dairy didn't feel special enough, and a quiche with the half and half and buttery crust was too rich. We fell in love with a crustless quiche. I also tried lots of cheeses. The Gruyére won in the end, but Mr. Goat was close behind.

2 tablespoons (¼ stick) unsalted butter

2 cups 1-inch diagonal pieces trimmed asparagus spears

1 large leek, white and pale green parts only, cut in half lengthwise, then thinly sliced crosswise (about 1 cup)

8 large eggs

2 cups half and half

1 teaspoon ground nutmeg

¼ teaspoon kosher salt

¼ teaspoon freshly ground black pepper

1½ cups coarsely grated Gruyére cheese

3 tablespoons chopped fresh dill

Position the rack in the center of the oven and preheat to 350°F. Butter a 9-inch glass deep-dish pie dish. Melt 2 tablespoons butter in a heavy medium skillet over medium-high heat. Add the asparagus and leek and sauté until the vegetables are almost tender, 4 to 5 minutes. Remove from the heat. Spread the vegetables evenly in the prepared pie dish.

Vigorously whisk the eggs, half and half, nutmeg, salt, and pepper in a large bowl to blend. Pour the egg mixture over the vegetables. Sprinkle the cheese over the eggs, then evenly sprinkle the dill over the cheese.

Bake the quiche until set, puffed, and lightly golden on top. Tent the quiche with foil halfway through baking if browning too quickly, 45 to 55 minutes total. Remove the quiche from the oven and cool slightly. Cut into wedges and serve warm, or serve at room temperature.

A lovely gift is lavender sugar. It's wonderful for baking or for sprinkling on yogurt. Use ½ cup dried lavender flowers to 6 cups sugar. Stir together and put in beautiful glass jars.

Triple berry upside down cake

I love the novelty of flipping the cake and seeing the maze of berries on the top. A dish like this makes me feel like I can accomplish things even when life doesn't. You can use all one kind of berry or add an herb to switch it up. Always taste the berries for tartness, and adjust the sugar as needed.

1 cup fresh blackberries

1 cup fresh blueberries

1 cup fresh raspberries

3 tablespoons powdered sugar

2¼ cups all-purpose flour

1½ teaspoons baking powder

1 teaspoon sea salt

½ teaspoon baking soda

1 cup whole milk

1 tablespoon fresh lime juice

2 teaspoons vanilla extract

12 taplespoons (1½ sticks) unsalted butter, softened

1⅓ cups sugar

3 large eggs

Powdered sugar (for sifting)

Finely grated lime zest (for garnish)

Position the rack in the center of the oven and preheat to 350°F. Butter two round 8-inch cake pans with 1½-inch high sides. Line the bottom of the pans with parchment paper, butter and flour.

Combine all the berries in a medium bowl. Add 3 tablespoons powdered sugar and toss gently to coat. Divide the berry mixture equally between the prepared pans, arranging in an even layer. Set aside.

Whisk the flour, baking powder, salt, and baking soda in another medium bowl to blend.

Mix the milk with the lime juice, creating buttermilk, and add vanilla in a small bowl.

Using an electric mixer, beat the butter and sugar in a large bowl until light and fluffy. Add the eggs, 1 at a time, beating well after each addition. Add the flour mixture in 3 additions, alternately with the buttermilk mixture in 2 additions, beginning and ending with the flour mixture and beating just until blended. Spoon the batter evenly over the berries in the pans.

Bake the cakes until a tester inserted into the center of the cakes comes out clean, 40 to 45 minutes. Transfer the cakes to a rack and cool completely in the pans. Invert each cake onto a plate. Remove the parchment paper. Sift powdered sugar generously over each cake. Garnish with a sprinkling of lime zest. Cut the cake into wedges and serve.

Bar was a bust

This menu is inspired by that night when friends pop by at the last minute or those nights at the bar that just never get going. Bring some revelry into your kitchen and invite your friends back to your place. All of these ingredients have shelf lives because this is a last-minute throw-together dinner party. Even if the bar was a bust, it doesn't mean you can't have a great night with your friends.

PARTY OF 4

Goat Cheese with Olive Tapenade 188

Spinach Salad with Pancetta 188

Roasted Tomato Linguine 190

Lemon Sgroppino 193

Goat cheese with olive tapenade

Pull the olives out of the cupboard, chop them up, and drizzle with olive oil. Add some herbs—done.

One 4- to 5-ounce soft fresh
    goat cheese log

½ cup olives

½ teaspoon herbs de provence

Extra-virgin olive oil

Crackers and/or baguette slices

Place the goat cheese log on a serving plate. Finely chop up olives or sundried tomatoes to make a quick tapenade. Mix in herbs. Spoon on top of cheese and drizzle with olive oil. Serve with crackers and baguette slices.

Spinach salad with pancetta

SERVES 4

Pancetta keeps forever in your fridge. It adds a saltiness that makes spinach salad more interesting.

One 3-ounce package thinly
    sliced pancetta

2 tablespoons fresh lemon juice

4 teaspoons balsamic vinegar

⅓ cup extra-virgin olive oil

Sea salt and freshly ground
    black pepper, to taste

One 5-ounce package baby
    spinach leaves

Preheat the oven to 450°F. Arrange the pancetta slices in a single layer on a large rimmed baking sheet. Bake until the pancetta is brown and crisp, 5 to 8 minutes. Remove from the oven. Transfer the pancetta to paper towels to drain. Coarsely crumble the pancetta and set aside.

Whisk the lemon juice and vinegar in a small bowl. Add the olive oil and whisk until well blended and emulsified. Season the vinaigrette to taste with salt and freshly ground black pepper.

Place the spinach in a large serving bowl. Drizzle the vinaigrette over the spinach. Crumble the pancetta over the spinach and serve.

Roasted tomato linguine

SERVES 4

My dear neighbor Franca is a legendary Italian cook. One of the best parts of living in our neighborhood is getting to indulge in all her Italian delicacies that she whips up with ease. I asked her what native Italians would make on a random night when they have a last-minute dinner to whip up. This dish is quick and wonderful.

---

1 pound cherry tomatoes

¼ cup extra-virgin olive oil

8 whole garlic cloves, peeled

2 teaspoons sugar

½ cup dried bread crumbs

1 tablespoon dried Italian seasoning

1½ teaspoons kosher salt

16 ounces linguine

Fresh basil leaves, for garnish

Preheat the oven to 450°F. Toss the tomatoes, olive oil, garlic, and sugar in a 2-quart broiler-proof baking dish.

Mix the bread crumbs, Italian seasoning, and salt in a small bowl. Sprinkle the bread crumb mixture over the tomatoes. Bake until the tomatoes begin to soften, about 15 minutes. Remove the dish with the tomatoes from the oven and preheat the broiler. Broil the tomatoes until brown and blistered in spots, about 5 minutes. Remove from the broiler.

Meanwhile, cook the linguine in a large pot of boiling salted water until just tender but still firm to bite. Drain. Return the linguine to the pot. Add the tomato mixture to the linguine and toss. Transfer the pasta to a large bowl. Garnish with basil leaves and serve.

Lemon sgroppino

This is an Italian recipe, and it is meant to be a dessert, not a cocktail. It usually has a splash of prosecco, so add it if you have it. If you've run out of champers like I always do, just make it with vodka. It is so refreshing. Sliver some mint on the top.

1⅓ cups lemon sorbet

½ cup vodka

Chilled prosecco (optional)

Mint, for garnish

Combine the lemon sorbet and the vodka in a medium bowl. Whisk gently until blended. Divide the mixture among 4 glasses. If desired, add a splash of prosecco to each glass and serve immediately. Garnish with mint.

june

"At first glance it may appear too hard.

Look again. Always look again."

Wine tasting evening

The first time I ever threw a wine tasting was to celebrate my brother-in-law's engagement. I had no idea what I was doing but happened to come across a young sommelier who was willing to work the party and teach me a thing or two about wines. It's so fun to learn about wine and experiment with food pairing. It makes you feel all grown up. From the bouillabaisse to the plum tarte tatin, this menu calls for an elegant night. Enlist the help of your friends by assigning them a bottle of wine to bring.

PARTY OF 10

French Wine Tasting with Pairings 198

Wine Pairings 199

Bouillabaisse with Saffron Aioli Crostini 201

Salted Caramel Plum Tarte Tatin 204

French wine tasting with pairings

The wines in this tasting are all French because the whole evening was inspired by bouillabaisse. Research the region where your dish is from and pair it with a wine from that area. Use your local wine store as a resource and ask them about the smaller vineyards around the world. They often produce some of the best wines.

First Tasting: Champagne
The first tasting is best when it's champagne. It ripens the palette and stimulates the appetite.

Second Tasting: Sancerre
The second tasting is a white wine, my favorite being a Sancerre. Sancerres get their name from a village in the Loire Valley of France, the surrounding vineyard of which provides grapes for this delicious wine. Try to find one with balanced grapefruit and gooseberry notes.

Third Tasting: Rosé
Round three is the rosé round. I adore blush rosés from Provence. After the first two tasting rounds, this is the time you want an element of refreshment with a wine that has a light acidity. This is the wine I serve with my bouillabaisse dinner.

Fourth Tasting: Saint-Émilion
Saint-Émilion is by far my favorite merlot. I could skip the whole tasting and only pour this bottle, that's how good it is. There are some big differences. If you want something with more acidity then look for an older vintage.

Fifth Tasting: Banyuls
We didn't make it to the fifth tasting but if you do then choose a Banyuls, a French port. This dessert wine is lovely served with the plum tarte tartin.

Wine pairings

SERVES 10

Pair the champagne with the smoked trout.

One 750-ml bottle chilled brut champagne

4 to 5 ounces smoked trout, broken into 1-inch pieces

Pair the Sancerre with the Boucheron goat cheese.

One 750-ml bottle slightly chilled Sancerre

4 to 5 ounces Boucheron goat cheese, broken into bite-size chunks

Pair the rosé with the fennel salami.

Three 750-ml bottles chilled rosé

4 to 5 ounces fennel salami, cut crosswise into 10 slices

Pair the Saint-Émilion with the dark chocolate.

One 750-ml bottle Saint-Émilion

4 to 5 ounces dark chocolate, broken into 10 pieces

Pair the Banyuls with the Stilton cheese.

One 750-ml bottle Banyuls

4 to 5 ounces Stilton cheese, broken into bite-size chunks

Serve the remaining rosé with the dinner.

Bouillabaisse with saffron aioli crostini

SERVES 10

As the epitome of elegance, this dish is perfect for special occasions. A bouillabaisse is a fish stew originating from the port city of Marseille. To me, there are two important elements to this dish, the saffron and the flavor that comes from a homemade broth made with the fish bones, shells, and skins. I make the broth the night before so that I can have more time with my guests. Bon Appetit!

SAFFRON AIOLI

1½ teaspoons fresh lemon juice

½ teaspoon crumbled saffron threads

¾ cup mayonnaise

3 tablespoons extra-virgin olive oil

2 large garlic cloves, peeled and pressed

BOUILLABAISSE

2½ pounds white potatoes

¾ cup extra-virgin olive oil

3 leeks (white parts only), well rinsed, coarsely chopped

1 fennel bulb, coarsely chopped

1 large onion, coarsely chopped

6 cloves garlic, coarsely chopped

To make the saffron aioli: Dissolve saffron in the lemon juice in a small glass bowl. Then mix in mayonnaise, olive oil, and garlic. (Saffron Aioli can be made 1 week ahead. Cover and refrigerate).

To make the bouillabaisse: Place potatoes in a medium saucepan of cold water. Bring to a boil over high heat. Continue boiling until a knife pierces the potato centers easily, about 20 minutes. Cool the potatoes, then peel. Cut potatoes into ⅓-inch thick rounds. (Potatoes can be prepared 2 days ahead. Cover and refrigerate. Bring to room temperature before using.)

Heat oil in a very large wide pot over medium heat. Add leeks, fennel, onion, garlic, saffron, dried red pepper, thyme, parsley, and bay leaves. Cook over medium heat until the vegetables soften, but do not brown, stirring occasionally, about 10 minutes. Add water, wine, clam juice, tomatoes, tomato paste, lobster shells, and shrimp shells and bring to a boil. Reduce heat and simmer for 15 minutes.

Set a large strainer over a large bowl. Pour the shellfish mixture into the strainer. Press on the solids with the back of a large spoon, releasing as much liquid as possible. (Shellfish broth can be made 1 day ahead. Refrigerate uncovered until cold, then cover and keep refrigerated.)

(continued)

1½ teaspoons crumbled saffron threads

¾ teaspoon dried red pepper flakes

10 fresh thyme sprigs

6 fresh parsley sprigs

3 bay leaves

3 quarts water

1½ cups dry white wine

12 ounces bottled clam juice or fish stock

9 plum tomatoes, coarsely chopped

6 tablespoons tomato paste

2 lobster tails, shells removed and reserved, lobster meat cut into 1-inch pieces

30 large uncooked shrimp, peeled, deveined, end of tails left intact, shells reserved

3 tablespoons Pernod or Ricard

30 mussels, scrubbed, de-bearded

30 littleneck clams, scrubbed

1½ pound snapper, cut into 2-inch pieces

1½ pound halibut, cut into 2-inch pieces

1 loaf pane rustica bread, thinly sliced crosswise, toasted

Pour the shellfish broth into the same large pot. Add Pernod and bring to a boil. Add mussels and clams. Cover and cook over high heat until the mussel and clam shells open, about 4 minutes. Discard any shells that do not open. Using a slotted spoon, transfer clams and mussels to a large bowl, covered. Add fish, shrimp, and lobster to the broth and cook over low heat until the fish is opaque in the center, about 4 minutes. Season to taste with salt.

Divide sliced potatoes with mussels and clams among 10 large shallow bowls. Ladle soup over the potatoes. Spread aioli over slices of toast and place atop soup. Serve immediately.

⟞ **There are many ways I have served this dish—as a refined plated dinner or with the help of all guests standing around the island in my kitchen. A bit of wine and lots of laughs helped me to dole out tasks. Everyone loves being part of preparing the meal.**

⟞ **Ask your fish monger to remove the shrimp and lobster from the shells and skin the fish for you, and reserve them separately. The shells will be simmered in the broth, adding a rich depth of flavor.**

Salted caramel plum tarte tatin

1 TARTE

This is an ooey-gooey tarte tatin. Traditionally it's made with apples, but I think plums with caramel is quite special. This recipe was by far the most delicious and difficult one to develop. The obstacle being the varying ripeness of the fruit—the juice content of the plums gave off too much liquid. We tried tapioca starch, sweating the plums, and precooking the plums, but decided that the best way is to remove a bit of juice at the end and to use firm plums. People swoon over this dessert.

1 cup sugar

¼ cup ruby Port or Banyuls

2½ tablespoons unsalted butter

¼ teaspoon flaked salt

2 pounds firm plums, halved and pitted

1 frozen puff pastry sheet, thawed

Position the oven rack in the center of the oven and preheat to 400°F.

Combine the sugar and Port in a heavy small saucepan. Stir over medium-low heat until the sugar dissolves. Increase the heat to high and boil without stirring until the syrup is a deep amber color, occasionally swirling the skillet, about 6 minutes. Immediately remove the saucepan from the heat and add the butter, 1 tablespoon at a time, then the salt, whisking to incorporate. Carefully pour the caramel into a 10-inch-diameter cast iron skillet and quickly spread evenly with a spatula (use extreme caution as the caramel is as hot as molten lava). Caramel will harden immediately.

Arrange the plums, cut side down, closely together in concentric circles atop the caramel in the skillet (the plums will shrink as they cook).

Roll out the puff pastry on a lightly floured surface and cut into a 12-inch round. Place the puff pastry round atop the plums in the skillet. Tuck the pastry edges down between the plums and the sides of the skillet, covering the plums completely. Using a fork, pierce the pastry in several places to allow steam to escape while baking. Place in the oven and bake the tarte tatin until the pastry is golden brown and cooked through and the plum juices are bubbling around the sides of the skillet, about 20 minutes. Remove from the oven. Using an oven mitt gently tilt the skillet. With a turkey baster, remove excess juices from the tarte tatin (a few tablespoons and up to ½ cup). Allow the tarte to cool in the skillet while the juices set, at least 30 minutes.

When ready to serve, reheat tarte on medium-high heat for one minute to loosen tarte.

Place a rimmed platter atop the skillet. Using oven mitts, hold the skillet and the platter firmly together and turn the skillet over, allowing the tarte tatin to settle onto the platter. Cut into wedges and serve.

El diablo

I call this party El Diablo, one because it's spicy and two because it was hell to make. When Hayes finished a movie, we hosted a wrap party. I needed to feed a crowd but I was developing the menu on the fly so I was behind the stove the entire night and didn't get to be a good hostess or wife. I didn't test anything beforehand and I'll tell you that cooking for sixteen is not the time to be adjusting spice mixtures. Nothing was served until almost ten at night. Lesson learned: plan ahead and don't be afraid to ask for a sous chef. That being said, I tweaked these recipes without a house full of rowdy actors. They are also great halved for a weekend fiesta.

PARTY OF 16

Jalapeño Margarita   208

Guacamole Salsa   208

Poblano Chorizo Quesadillas   209

Mahi mahi Tacos with Nectarine Salsa   212

Slaw with Toasted Pepitas   215

Tequila-Marinated Grilled Pineapple   215

Jalapeño margarita

SERVES 16

Deb is a fabulous hostess, and this is her signature spicy margarita that she serves at her fiestas all summer long. Brace yourself—it brings a bit of heat into the party.

SPICY TEQUILA

One 750-ml bottle premium tequila

1 jalapeño chile, cut in half lengthwise with seeds intact

JALAPEÑO MARGARITA
(1 serving)

2 ounces spicy tequila

2 tablespoons fresh lime juice

1 tablespoon Cointreau

1 teaspoon agave syrup

Ice cubes

To make the spicy tequila: Open the tequila bottle and drop the jalapeño in. Cover with the bottle cap and let flavors infuse for at least 1 day and up to 3 days.

To make each jalapeño margarita: combine ¼ cup spicy tequila, 2 tablespoons lime juice, 2 tablespoons water, 1 tablespoon Cointreau, 1 teaspoon agave syrup and ½ cup ice cubes in a cocktail shaker. Shake vigorously for 30 seconds.

Fill a rocks glass with fresh ice cubes. Strain the margarita over the ice cubes and serve.

Guacamole salsa

SERVES 16

Everyone dips from the guacamole into the salsa anyway, right?

---

8 large ripe avocados, peeled, pitted, coarsely chopped

1½ cups salsa verde

3 tablespoons sour cream

½ teaspoon garlic salt

Tortilla chips

Place the avocados in a large bowl. Mash coarsely with a fork. Stir in the salsa verde, sour cream, and garlic salt. Serve with tortilla chips.

Poblano chorizo quesadillas

SERVES 16

I used to be scared of cooking with chilies; they were so intimidating. When you roast a poblano chili and peel it, it's so delicious and adds an incredible flavor. Everyone grabs a quesadilla as soon as it's put out. They are gone in a flash!

---

4 large poblano or pasilla chilies

10 ounces Mexican-style chorizo

1 tablespoon cumin seeds

10 ounces grated Monterey Jack cheese

4 ounces feta cheese, crumbled

½ cup chopped fresh cilantro

¼ cup chopped fresh oregano

Picante sauce

Extra-virgin olive oil for brushing

Sixteen 5- to 6-inch round corn and/or flour tortillas

Char the chilies over a gas flame or under a broiler until blackened and charred on all sides. Transfer the chilies to a bowl and cover with plastic, allowing them to steam while cooling. Peel, seed, stem, and slice the chilies.

Cook the chorizo in a heavy medium skillet over medium heat until well browned, stirring occasionally, about 25 minutes.

Stir the cumin seeds in a heavy small skillet over medium high heat until lightly toasted, about 1 minute. Transfer to a large bowl to cool. Add both cheeses, cilantro, and oregano to the cumin in the bowl.

Heat a large skillet over medium heat on the barbecue grill or stove-top. Brush the skillet with olive oil. Warm one tortilla in the skillet. Sprinkle cheese mixture, chili strips, chorizo, and picante sauce onto tortilla. Fold the tortillas in half, enclosing the filling. Cook until the cheese melts and the tortilla browns slightly, turning once with tongs, about 4 minutes. Serve.

"I am certain of nothing
but the holiness of the
heart's affections, and
the truth of
imagination."

—John Keats

Mahi mahi tacos with nectarine salsa

SERVES 16

The flavors in this recipe fuse together to make a stand-out fish taco. The spice mixture is key to enliven the mahi mahi. You can substitute mangos or peaches for the nectarines, whichever is ripe in the market that day.

SALSA

6 ripe nectarines, halved, pitted, cut into ⅓-inch cubes

5 green onions, finely chopped

3 tablespoons finely chopped fresh cilantro

2 jalapeños, seeded, minced

¼ cup fresh lime juice (from about 2 limes)

¼ cup extra-virgin olive oil

CRÈME VERDE

Three 8-ounce containers crème fraîche

2 tablespoons green hot sauce

MAHI MAHI

¼ cup paprika

¼ cup garlic powder

4 teaspoons onion powder

4 teaspoons dried oregano

4 teaspoons kosher salt

2 teaspoons freshly ground black pepper

1 teaspoon cayenne pepper

5 pounds mahi mahi fillets

To make the salsa: Combine the nectarines, green onions, cilantro, and jalapeños in a medium bowl. Stir in the lime juice and olive oil. Season the salsa to taste with salt and pepper.

To make the crème verde: Stir the crème fraîche and the green hot sauce in a small bowl to blend well.

To make the mahi mahi: Mix all the spices in a small bowl. Place the fish fillets on a rimmed baking sheet. Brush the fish generously with olive oil or vegetable oil. Rub about half of the spice mixture generously over both sides of the fish fillets, reserving the remaining spice mixture for another use, like on chicken or shrimp. (The fish can be prepared up to 6 hours ahead. Cover and refrigerate.)

Prepare the grill for direct cooking over medium-high heat. Stack the tortillas in 2 stacks on 2 large pieces of foil and wrap each tightly to seal. Place the wrapped tortillas on one side of the grill and the fish on the other. Grill the fish fillets until just opaque in the center, turning once, about 7 to 8 minutes total, depending on thickness of the fillets. Transfer them and break the fish into small pieces.

Spread 1 tortilla with some of the crème verde; top with another tortilla. Fill the tortilla with fish and nectarine salsa. Repeat with remaining tortillas.

Olive oil or vegetable oil

Sixty-four 5- to 6-inch corn tortillas

⌐ When I am having a smaller group over, I usually plate them myself but with this large of a group, it's easiest to serve a platter of grilled fish and bowls filled with salsa and crème verde, and the guests can assemble the tacos themselves.

Slaw with toasted pepitas

SERVES 16

2 cups chopped red onion

1 cup fresh lime juice

1 cup grape seed oil

1 cup chopped fresh cilantro

3 tablespoons agave syrup

3 tablespoons lime zest

1¼ teaspoons sea salt

2 medium heads red cabbage, cored, thinly sliced

¾ cup salted pepitas (pumpkin seeds), lightly toasted

Combine the onion, lime juice, oil, cilantro, agave, and lime zest in a food processor. Puree until almost smooth and well blended. (The dressing can be prepared 24 hours ahead. Cover and refrigerate.)

Place the cabbage in a large bowl. Add the dressing and toss to coat. Season with salt and pepper. Transfer the slaw to a serving bowl. Sprinkle with the pepitas and serve. This bright citrusy slaw is a great partner to the tacos.

Tequila-marinated grilled pineapple

SERVES 16

Pineapple skewers are a fun dessert to round off the El Diablo party.

1 cup tequila

¾ cup packed brown sugar

1½ teaspoons vanilla extract

1 teaspoon ground cinnamon

½ teaspoon ground allspice

2 ripe pineapples, peeled, cored, cut into large chunks

16 wooden skewers, soaked in water for at least 1 hour before grilling, then drained

1½ cups Mascarpone cheese

Combine the tequila, brown sugar, vanilla, cinnamon, and allspice in a large glass bowl. Stir until the sugar dissolves. Add the pineapple and turn to coat with the marinade. Cover and refrigerate at least 1 hour.

Turn the grill on medium heat. Thread the pineapple chunks onto the skewers. Transfer the leftover marinade to a small saucepan and cook over medium heat until slightly reduced and thickened, stirring frequently, about 10 to 15 minutes. Remove from the heat. Cover to keep warm.

Grill the pineapple until slightly charred, turning occasionally, 5 to 7 minutes. Transfer to a platter. Serve the mascarpone and marinade sauce alongside.

july

Americana bbq

July is about making the most of the long warm days and a barbecue is a pure American way of doing so. This menu has all the classic flavors but with a light fresh twist. It's about great friends and easygoing dishes with time to chase the fireflies.

PARTY OF 8

Tequila, Lime, Agave, and Club Soda   221

Summer Tomatoes with Crumbled Bleu   221

Chicken with Jersey Peach BBQ Sauce   222

French Potato Salad   224

Grilled Asparagus and Portobello Mushrooms   225

Blueberry Crumble   227

Tequila, lime, agave, and club soda

SERVES 8

*My girlfriend Kasey is one of my favorite friends to have a cocktail with.
She introduced me to this light effervescent concoction.*

Ice cubes

2 cups tequila

2 cups fresh lime juice

½ cup agave syrup

4 cups chilled club soda

Fill 8 rocks glasses with ice cubes. Pour tequila, lime juice, and agave syrup, and club soda into a large pitcher. Stir to mix, fill each glass, and serve.

Summer tomatoes with crumbled bleu

SERVES 8

*I adore tomatoes with cheese. This recipe calls for a sun-ripened tomato
with crumbles of creamy salty blue cheese and a splash of balsamic.
Simple perfection.*

4 large heirloom tomatoes of assorted colors, thickly sliced

¼ of a large red onion, thinly sliced

6 ounces good-quality bleu cheese (such as Point Reyes), coarsely crumbled

Extra-virgin olive oil for drizzling

Balsamic vinegar, for drizzling

Flaked sea salt and freshly ground black pepper, to taste

Arrange the tomatoes on a serving platter. Scatter the onion slices over the tomatoes. Sprinkle with the bleu cheese. Drizzle the tomatoes lightly with olive oil and balsamic vinegar. Sprinkle lightly with sea salt and cracked pepper and serve.

Chicken with jersey peach bbq sauce

MAKES 3 CUP

I used to buy barbecue sauces but recently found out they were really easy to make. So get bragging rights, especially with this one layered with flavor from the peaches, brown sugar, and jalapeños.

SAUCE

2 tablespoons olive oil

1 ½ cups finely chopped onion

2 small garlic cloves, peeled and minced

1½ pounds ripe peaches, un-peeled, pitted, and coarsely chopped or frozen

¾ cup apple cider vinegar

⅓ cup packed dark brown sugar

3 tablespoons bourbon

3 tablespoons concentrated tomato paste

1 scant teaspoon chili powder

½ teaspoon kosher salt

½ teaspoon freshly ground black pepper

¼ teaspoon cayenne pepper

1 tablespoon minced, seeded jalapeños

CHICKEN

8 bone-in, skin-on chicken breast halves

Extra-virgin olive oil, for brushing

To make the sauce: Heat the oil in a heavy 2-quart saucepan over medium-high heat. Add the onion and sauté until tender and golden brown, about 8 minutes. Stir in the garlic and cook until the garlic is fragrant, about 1 minute. Stir in the peaches, vinegar, brown sugar, bourbon, tomato paste, chili powder, salt, pepper, and cayenne. Reduce the heat to medium and simmer until the peaches fall apart and the mixture has thickened slightly, about 25 minutes. Cool the mixture slightly. Transfer the peach mixture to a blender and puree until smooth. Stir in minced jalapeño.

To make the chicken: Prepare the barbecue to medium-high heat. Brush both sides of the chicken breasts with olive oil and sprinkle with salt and pepper. Arrange the chicken on the grill and cook until browned on both sides, turning once, about 10 minutes total. Turn one or two burners off. Move the chicken to indirect heat. Close the barbecue and continue cooking until the chicken is almost cooked through, about 10 minutes longer. Brush the chicken thickly with the sauce; cover and cook until sauce sets, about 2 minutes, each side. Transfer the chicken to a platter and serve.

French potato salad

This warm potato salad was inspired by Jacques Pépin's classic dish. The mustard and vinegar create a nice tang! No worries about leaving this dish out; it is supposed to be room temp to warm to let flavors meld.

DRESSING

½ cup dry white wine

3 tablespoons champagne vinegar or white wine vinegar

3 tablespoons plus ⅓ cup extra-virgin olive oil, divided

¼ cup finely chopped fresh chives or green onion tops

3 tablespoons chopped fresh Italian parsley

2 tablespoons chopped fresh tarragon (from about 1 bunch)

1 teaspoon sea salt

1 teaspoon freshly ground black pepper

1 cup chopped white onion (from about 1 small)

1 cup chopped green onions, white and pale green parts only

5 medium garlic cloves, peeled and pressed

POTATOES

2 pounds small waxy potatoes (such as fingerlings), cut into ⅓-inch-thick rounds

8 ounces haricots verts or other slender green beans, trimmed, halved crosswise

To make the dressing: Whisk the white wine, vinegar, and 3 tablespoons olive oil in a small bowl to blend. Whisk in the chives, parsley, tarragon, 1 teaspoon salt, and 1 teaspoon pepper. Set aside.

Heat the remaining ⅓ cup olive oil in a heavy medium skillet over medium-high heat. Add the onion and sauté until tender and golden, 3 to 5 minutes. Add the green onions and garlic and stir until fragrant and the green onions are just wilted, about 2 minutes. Remove from the heat. Stir the warm onion mixture into the vinegar-herb mixture. Set the dressing aside while cooking the potatoes.

To make the potatoes: Cook the potatoes in a large pot of boiling salted water until just barely tender, 10 to 12 minutes. During the last 2 to 3 minutes of cooking the potatoes, add the haricots verts to the pot and cook just until the haricots verts are crisp-tender. Drain well. Transfer the potatoes and haricots verts to a large bowl. Immediately add the dressing to the warm potato mixture and toss very gently to prevent the potatoes from breaking. If desired, adjust the seasoning with more salt and pepper and serve while still warm.

Grilled asparagus and portobello mushrooms

SERVES 8

You never know when a vegetarian/vegan/gluten-free guest will show up at your table, so here is a worry-free dish. Buy whatever vegetables look the freshest and tastiest. Summer flavors, simply made.

2 bunches asparagus (about 1½ pounds total), tough ends trimmed

4 portobello mushrooms, stems trimmed and discarded

3 medium zucchini, trimmed, cut lengthwise into ¼-inch thick slices

½ cup extra-virgin olive oil

2 tablespoons herbs de provence

Brush the vegetables all over with olive oil. Sprinkle with salt, pepper, and herbs de provence.

Grill the vegetables over medium heat until just tender and grill marks appear, turning once, about 5 minutes for the asparagus and zucchini, and about 8 minutes for the mushrooms. Transfer to a platter and serve.

⌒ **For herbed corn, simmer a large pot of salted water and add husked corn for 5 minutes. Remove and slather with herbed butter.**

Blueberry crumble

SERVES 8

Hey reveler, this is essential. You should trust and honor your palate. I like to let the real flavor of the fruit shine, but I always taste the berries and sweeten it to my liking. The reason I love this crumble is the oatmeal almond topping. It goes with any fruit, such as blackberries or mixed with peaches. My friends serve it to their kids for a healthy breakfast with a dollop of greek yogurt.

TOPPING

¾ cup all purpose flour

¾ cup quick-cooking oats

½ cup packed brown sugar

½ cup coarsely chopped almonds (about 2 ounces)

¾ teaspoon kosher salt

1 teaspoon vanilla extract

½ teaspoon ground cinnamon

¼ teaspoon ground nutmeg

½ cup (1 stick) unsalted butter, cut into ½-inch cubes, softened

FILLING

½ cup sugar

¼ cup all-purpose flour

¼ teaspoon kosher salt

Two 12-ounce baskets fresh blueberries

2 tablespoons fresh lemon juice

Vanilla ice cream

To make the topping: Combine the flour, oats, brown sugar, almonds, salt, vanilla, cinnamon, and nutmeg in a medium bowl. Add the butter and rub in with your fingertips until moist clumps form.

To make the filling: Position the rack in the center of the oven and preheat to 375°F. Butter a 9-inch pie dish. Whisk the sugar, flour, and salt in a large bowl to blend. Add the blueberries and lemon juice to the sugar mixture and toss gently with a silicone spatula to coat, being careful not to break the berries. Transfer the berry mixture to the prepared pie dish. Sprinkle the topping evenly over the filling.

Bake the crumble until the filling is bubbling thickly at the edges and the topping is crisp and golden brown, 45 to 50 minutes. Transfer the dish to a rack and let it set, about 15 minutes. Serve with scoops of vanilla ice cream.

Dinner at dusk

This dinner is for my honey because he loves our meals at home. Set the table and leave the lighting to nature. Serve with lillet, a lovely French spritzer that is hard to resist when you're cooking on a hot summer afternoon. Mix lillet with sparkling water and a squeeze of lime. A perfect way to start a party whether it's for 2 or 20.

PARTY OF 2

Halibut with Romesco Sauce 230

Zucchini Carpaccio with Manchego 234

Berries with Spiked Whip 234

Halibut with romesco sauce

SERVES 6 WITH EXTRA SAUCE

*I am always looking for interesting sauces to man-up dishes. This
Spanish sauce is usually made with raw almonds, but I enjoy the richness
of Marconas. Both are delicious. The halibut stands up to the sauce and
cooks simply in the same pan as the potatoes.*

ROMESCO SAUCE

1 large dried ancho chile

2 large red bell peppers or 2
    roasted peppers from a jar

3 plum tomatoes, cut in half
    lengthwise

1 cup 1-inch cubes sourdough
    bread

4 garlic cloves, peeled

1½ teaspoons plus ½ cup
    extra-virgin olive oil,
    divided

¼ cup Marcona almonds

2 tablespoons sherry wine
    vinegar

1 tablespoon fresh lemon juice

4 teaspoons smoked paprika

¼ teaspoon sea salt

¼ teaspoon freshly ground
    black pepper

HALIBUT

2 tablespoons olive oil, divided

½ pound baby potatoes (about
    1 to 1½ inches long), halved
    lengthwise

To make the romesco sauce: Place the ancho chili in a small bowl.
Pour enough hot water over to cover the chile. Let soak until the chile
is very soft, about 30 minutes. Drain. Remove the stem and seeds
from the chili and discard.

Preheat the broiler. Place the bell peppers on a rimmed baking sheet.
Broil until charred and blackened on all sides, turning occasionally,
about 15 minutes. Transfer the peppers to a bowl; cover with plastic
wrap and let steam 15 to 20 minutes. Peel, seed, and coarsely chop
the peppers.

Preheat the oven to 375°F. Toss the tomatoes, bread cubes, and garlic
with 1½ teaspoons olive oil in a medium bowl to lightly coat. Spread on
a rimmed baking sheet and bake until tomatoes are slightly softened,
about 15 minutes. Add the chili to the baking sheet and continue to
bake 3 to 4 minutes longer. Remove from the oven.

Pulse the bell peppers, tomato-bread-and-chili mixture, almonds,
vinegar, lemon juice, smoked paprika, salt, and pepper in a food
processor. Then, slowly add remaining ½ cup olive oil. Blend until the
mixture is almost smooth. Transfer to a bowl.

To make the halibut: Turn the oven on to 450°F.

Toss the potatoes with 1 tablespoon olive oil, salt and pepper on a
rimmed baking sheet. Roast the potatoes in the oven for 10 minutes.

Two 6-ounce fresh halibut fillets, each about 1 inch thick

2 teaspoons minced fresh thyme

Kosher salt and freshly ground black pepper, to taste

Romesco Sauce (see recipe)

Brush the halibut fillets with remaining olive oil and sprinkle with thyme, salt, and pepper.

Remove the potato pan from the oven. Using a spatula, push the potatoes to one side of the baking sheet, and add the halibut to the hot pan. Roast the potatoes until they are golden brown and the halibut is just cooked through, about 7 minutes. Divide the halibut and potatoes among the plates. Spoon the romesco sauce atop the fish and serve. (There will be extra romesco sauce, which is great with crudités or grilled shrimp.)

Zucchini carpaccio with manchego

SERVES 2

Reveler, you'd be surprised how wonderful raw zucchini can be. By slivering it you get a delicate texture and an elegant look. The Manchego is a perfect cheese to pair with the Spanish romesco.

2 medium zucchini, trimmed, cut in half lengthwise

4 ounces Manchego cheese, coarsely crumbled

2 tablespoons pine nuts, lightly toasted

2 tablespoons extra-virgin olive oil

2 to 3 tablespoons fresh lemon juice

Flaked sea salt and freshly ground black pepper, to taste

Holding a vegetable peeler parallel to the cut surface of one zucchini half, thinly shave the zucchini half into long strips. Repeat with the remaining zucchini halves. Divide the zucchini strips between 2 serving plates, mounding the strips decoratively in the center of each plate. Sprinkle each with the cheese and the pine nuts, dividing equally. Drizzle each with the olive oil, then the lemon juice. Sprinkle lightly with flaked sea salt and freshly cracked pepper and serve.

Berries with spiked whip

SERVES 2

Berries with whipped cream is the perfect ending to any meal especially in the summer.

¾ cup chilled heavy whipping cream

2 tablespoons Lillet

1 tablespoon sugar

2 cups mixed fresh berries (such as blackberries, raspberries, and hulled strawberries)

Using an electric mixer, beat the cream, Lillet, and sugar in a medium bowl until soft peaks form (do not overbeat or the cream will curdle).

Divide the berries between 2 bowls. Spoon the Lillet-spiked whipped cream over the berries in each bowl and serve.

august

"In a sea of people,
my eyes will
always search for you."

Midsummer night's dream

This is my favorite party of the year; the days are long, the weather is warm, and produce is at its most flavorful. It is about great friends, bare feet, fabulous food, and the hope that the night will never end.

PARTY OF 12

Rosé Champagne with Vodka-Infused Raspberries 241

Fig , Prosciutto, and Mascarpone Crostini 242

Heirloom Tomato and Burrata Bruschetta 245

Lamb Chop Lollipops 247

Ratatouille with Parmagiano-Reggiano 248

Strawberry Mint Cake 249

Rosé champagne with vodka-infused raspberries

MAKES 12 SERVINGS

The vibe of this whole party starts with this drink, the origins of which come from the Hemingway Bar in Paris. As part of my bachelorette party, my friend Nancy had this cocktail created for me. Drinking this always reminds me of that glamorous trip. I love the way the raspberries add color to the champagne and cause it to sparkle. Plan ahead and infuse the raspberries at least three days in advance for the perfect drink.

Two 6-ounce packages fresh raspberries

2 cups vodka (1 pint)

Two 750-ml bottles chilled rosé champagne

Place the raspberries in a glass jar. Pour the vodka over the berries and cover with the lid to seal. Refrigerate at least 3 days and up to 2 weeks to allow the berries to absorb the vodka flavor.

Spoon 3 vodka-infused raspberries and 1 tablespoon of the raspberry vodka into each of 12 champagne glasses. Fill each glass with champagne and serve.

Fig, prosciutto, and mascarpone crostini

SERVES 12

I love appetizers that are simple to make but still have a sophisticated flavor. Someone always leaves with the recipe. This is also delicious with peaches or blackberries—whatever is in season.

CROSTINI

1 baguette, cut on slight diagonal into 24 slices

¼ cup extra-virgin olive oil

¾ cup mascarpone cheese (about 6 ounces)

8 ounces thinly sliced prosciutto

SYRUP

6 ripe fresh figs, stemmed, each cut crosswise into 6 slices

Balsamic syrup, for drizzling

Freshly ground black pepper, to taste

1 cup balsamic vinegar

1 tablespoon brown sugar

To make the crostini: Preheat the oven to 425°F. Arrange the baguette slices in a single layer on a large baking sheet. Brush the baguette slices lightly with olive oil. Bake until the slices are lightly golden brown, about 10 minutes. Remove from the oven and let the crostini cool to room temperature on the baking sheet.

Spread the mascarpone cheese over the crostini, dividing equally. Top each with a lightly folded slice of prosciutto, then a fig slice. Drizzle each generously with balsamic syrup and sprinkle lightly with cracked pepper and serve immediately.

To make the balsamic syrup: combine vinegar and sugar in a small saucepan, bring to a boil over medium heat. Stir occasionally for 5 minutes or until it's thick enough to coat the back of a spoon.

Heirloom tomato and burrata bruschetta

SERVES 12

I'm not sure there's anything better than an heirloom tomato with a dollop of burrata cheese. This is my deconstructed version of a classic Caprese salad. It is more than just an appetizer; on a lazy summer night, it's dinner. I grill or pan-fry pounded chicken breasts with fresh herbs and top with this heavenly mixture.

6 cups ½-inch sliced heirloom tomatoes (from about 8 large tomatoes)

½ cup plus 2 tablespoons extra-virgin olive oil, divided

2 large garlic cloves, peeled and minced

½ teaspoon flaked sea salt

½ teaspoon freshly ground black pepper

1 long baguette, cut on slight diagonal into ½-inch thick slices

16 ounces burrata cheese, drained

Fresh basil leaves, for garnish

Combine the tomatoes, ½ cup olive oil, garlic, sea salt, and pepper in a large bowl. Mix gently to blend. Cover and set aside at room temperature for up to 1 hour to allow the flavors to blend.

Position the rack in the center of the oven and preheat to 350°F. Arrange the baguette slices in a single layer on 2 large baking sheets, brush with remaining 2 tablespoons of olive oil. Bake at 350°F for 6 minutes.

On a large platter, spoon tomato mixture next to burrata and toasted baguette slices. Garnish with basil leaves.

Lamb chop lollipops

SERVES 12

This is one of my go-to party recipes. It is fast, easy, and a true show-stopper. You can prepare the herb mixture with the chops the day before. Keep the atmosphere casual and sexy by eating the lamb chops with your hands rather than a knife and fork. I love serving it '80s style against a mound of ratatouille. It's packed with flavor but not too heavy.

HERB RUB

10 garlic cloves, peeled and pressed

2 tablespoons finely chopped fresh rosemary

2 tablespoons finely chopped fresh thyme

1 tablespoon kosher salt

1 tablespoon whole black peppercorns

2 tablespoons extra-virgin olive oil

30 lamb rib chops, frenched, 2 to 3 ounces each

For the herb rub: Place the garlic, rosemary, thyme, salt, and peppercorns in a mortar with a pestle. Using the pestle, pound the herb mixture to a coarse paste. Mix in the olive oil. You can also pulse the mixture in a food processor.

For the lamb: Divide the lamb chops between 2 large baking sheets, arranging the chops in a single layer. Rub the herb mixture evenly onto the lamb chops. Cover the baking sheet with the lamb chops with plastic wrap and let sit for 30 minutes.

Position the oven rack in the upper third of the oven and preheat the broiler. Divide the lamb chops between 2 large baking sheets, arranging the chops in a single layer. Working with 1 baking sheet at a time, broil the lamb chops for 2 minutes. Turn the lamb chops over and broil on the second side until cooked to desired doneness, about 1 minute longer for medium-rare. Remove the chops from the oven. Repeat with the lamb chops on the second baking sheet. Place the lamb chops on a platter and serve.

Ratatouille with parmigiano-reggiano

SERVES 12

I think of ratatouille as a perfect combination of summer's greatest hits. Traditionally, it's prepared with eggplant and bell peppers, but my take is to add the sweetness of freshly shucked corn, and Parmigiano-Reggiano.

9 cups roma tomatoes cut into 1-inch cubes (from about 18 tomatoes)

3 tablespoons butter

3 tablespoons extra-virgin olive oil

3 cups diced onion

6 cloves garlic, peeled and minced

3 cups corn, (from about 6 ears of fresh)

9 cups zucchini, cut into ¾-inch cubes (from about 9 medium zucchini)

3 teaspoons sea salt

1½ teaspoons freshly ground black pepper

3½ cups Parmigiano-Reggiano cheese, shredded

Roughly chop and deseed tomatoes, set aside. Chop onions and sauté on medium-high heat in olive oil and butter for 5 minutes. Add garlic and continue to sauté for an additional 2 minutes. Add tomatoes and simmer for 15 minutes to reduce. Add corn, zucchini, salt, and pepper.

Turn the heat back up to medium for an additional 10 minutes. Turn off heat and stir in Parmigiano-Reggiano until melted, and serve.

Strawberry mint cake

SERVES 12

This is inspired by the legend Ina Garten. Ina has greatly influenced me and I consider her an OG (Original Gourmet). Her Strawberry Country Cake was one of the first cakes I ever made. I've changed it up a little over the years by using yogurt instead of sour cream and adding mint to the batter. It's a juicy, messier version, and I craved it throughout my entire pregnancy.

CAKE

4 large eggs

¾ cup plain Greek yogurt (do not use nonfat or low-fat)

1½ teaspoons vanilla extract

2 cups cake flour

1 teaspoon baking soda

½ teaspoon sea salt

¼ teaspoon cornstarch

2 cups sugar

12 tablespoons (1½ sticks) unsalted butter, room temperature

¼ cup fresh mint leaves, finely chopped

To make the cake: Position the rack in the center of the oven and preheat to 325°F. Butter two 8-inch round cake pans with 1½-inch-high sides. Dust the pans lightly with flour, tapping out excess flour.

Combine the eggs, yogurt, and vanilla in a medium bowl. Whisk to blend well. Combine the flour, baking soda, salt, and cornstarch in another medium bowl; whisk until blended. Combine the sugar and butter in a large bowl. Using an electric mixer, beat the sugar mixture on high speed until light and fluffy. Reduce the speed to medium and slowly add the egg mixture until well blended. Reduce the speed to low and gradually beat in the flour mixture until the batter is smooth. Stir in the fresh mint.

Divide the batter evenly between the prepared cake pans; smooth the tops. Lightly tap the pans on the work surface to allow the batter to settle evenly in the pans and to prevent air bubbles from forming. Bake the cakes until a tester inserted into the center of the cakes comes out clean, about 40 minutes. Remove the pans from the oven and transfer to a wire rack and allow the cakes to cool, 15 to 20 minutes in the pans. Run a small knife between the sides of the pans and the cakes to loosen. Invert a plate atop the pan of each cake. Hold the plate and cake pan firmly together and invert the cakes, allowing them to settle onto the plates. If necessary, tap the bottom of the pans to release the cakes. Remove the pans.

(continued)

FILLING

Two 16-ounce containers fresh strawberries, hulled, sliced, divided (save a few beauties to garnish top of cake)

Zest of ½ lemon (about 1 teaspoon)

1½ cups chilled heavy whipping cream

3 tablespoons sugar

½ teaspoon vanilla extract

To make the filling: Combine half of the strawberries and the lemon zest in a medium saucepan. Cook over low heat just until the berries are fragrant and softened slightly, about 2 minutes. Remove the saucepan from the heat. Transfer the berry mixture to a medium bowl and cool completely. Stir in the remaining strawberries.

Using an electric mixer, beat the whipping cream, 3 tablespoons sugar, and vanilla in a large bowl until medium-stiff peaks form. Do not overbeat.

To assemble: Place 1 cake on a platter. Arrange half of the strawberry mixture evenly atop the cake layer, allowing the strawberries to be visible at the edges of the cake (the juices from the berries will soak into the cake). Spread half of the whipped cream evenly over the strawberry mixture. Top with the second cake layer, then cover with the remaining strawberry mixture and whipped cream. Garnish with whole berries or sprigs of mint.

Tuesday night, no reason

This weeknight gathering is the essence of *Kitchen Revelry*. You can make up any excuse to entertain. No pressure to make it a big thing and get all stressed out. Stack some sandwiches on a cutting board, crack beers, and sit around the kitchen catching up. Why not? You got no other place to be except for work the next day.

PARTY OF 4

BLTs with Burrata and Pickled Onions 254

Melon Gazpacho 255

Berries with Spiked Whip (see page 234)

Blts with burrata and pickled onions

SERVES 6

Take your BLT to the next level. I headline these on my weekday party menu. My husband loves to have these while watching a game.

PICKLED ONIONS

¾ cup sugar

1½ cups red wine vinegar

1 tablespoon sea salt

1 large white onion, halved lengthwise, very thinly sliced

BLTS

18 slices thick cut bacon,

1 loaf sourdough, sliced

2 tablespoons extra-virgin olive oil

3 heirloom tomatoes, thickly sliced

16 ounces burrata cheese, drained

One 5-ounce package baby arugula

Flaked sea salt and freshly ground black pepper, to taste

To make the pickled onions: Combine the sugar, vinegar, and salt in a small saucepan. Bring to a boil, stirring over medium-high heat until the sugar dissolves. Remove the saucepan from the heat. Place the onion slices in a glass jar with a lid. Pour the vinegar mixture over the onions. Cover the jar with the lid and refrigerate at least 24 hours. (The pickled onions can be made up to 1 week ahead. Keep refrigerated.)

To make the BLTs: Working in batches, cook the bacon slices in a heavy large skillet over medium heat until brown and crisp. Transfer the bacon slices to paper towels to drain.

Lightly toast the bread. Before compiling your sandwiches, drizzle the bread with olive oil. Layer tomato, bacon, a dollop of burrata cheese, drained pickled onions, and arugula. Sprinkle lightly with sea salt and freshly ground black pepper and second bread slice.

Melon gazpacho

SERVES 6

It's a perfect snack during a hot summer night or a light dinner before a bikini day.

2 cups diced tomatoes

1 cup diced peeled seeded cucumber

¼ cup fresh lemon juice (from about 1 lemon)

¼ cup chopped fresh parsley

1 garlic clove, peeled and pressed

1 small shallot, chopped

½ cup diced, peeled, seeded honeydew melon or Cantelope

3 tablespoons extra-virgin olive oil

½ teaspoon sea salt

½ teaspoon freshly ground black pepper

Fresh parsley sprigs, for garnish

Combine the first 7 ingredients in a food processor. Blend to desired consistency, but be careful not to overblend or it will get frothy. Add the olive oil and blend 5 seconds longer. Season with salt and pepper, adding more to taste if desired. Refrigerate the gazpacho until cold, about 2 hours.

Ladle the gazpacho into 6 small bowls. I like to chop up some melon, and cucumber to garnish the top.

For a great finish, try these lime cup shooters. To prepare, cut your limes in half, hollow out most of the pulp, rim with salt, and fill with tequila. Then lick, shoot, and squeeze. They're amazing. (See page 252.)

For Tracy Zahoryin—From the day we met in Australia, our lives have been intertwined. Tracy was the first person to really introduce me to the beauty of "effortless entertaining." Her classic yet sexy style has inspired me and influenced me in countless ways. She has been a fundamental part of this book and it would not have been possible without her. From its conception, sitting on the deck drinking a glass of wine, to the long hours we have shared pounding out this book, I will always remember this as being one of the most extraordinary experiences of my life. Thank you for always being the voice of reason.

Acknowledgments

Michael Bircumshaw—My brilliant confidante, the fixer

Kathryn Huck—Patient, empowerer of creativity

Joy Tutela—Tireless champion

Danny Seo—The godfather, the first one to believe in this book

Amy Neunsinger—Coolest Cat, capturer of the moment

Alison Attenborough—The Legend

Kate Martindale—The Energizer Bunny

Sandra Cordero—The Kickass chef

Andy Mitchell—The Silent warrior

Steve Warren—My pitbull

Stephanie Gambino—Limitless talent

Lena Braun and Jeanne Kelly—Meticulous help for the newbie

Michele Kovach—Cinderella

Roxanna Alvarado—The mamabear, loved by all.

Susan Zahoryin—Gadimer, I love you

Rory Cochrane—2-28, thanks for sharing T

Mom and Dad—Belief in the beauty of dreams

Kris—My sister, my treasure

I am forever grateful to everyone who helped make this book a reality, including the team at St. Martin's Press for their dedication, and Dominique Appel, Lisa Jenkins, WME, and Artist & Brand for their constant support. A big thank-you to the beauty squad: Georgie Eisdell, Bridget Brager, and Christine Symonds. For their generosity, a thank-you to Perrier-Jouët, One Kings Lane, Heath Ceramics, Bed Head Pajamas, and Home Goods. To all my friends and family who showed up at the drop of a hat, no questions asked, looking as fabulous as ever, and were game to be part of this dream of mine—a big kiss.

Index

A

Agua Fresca, *24*, 25
Almond Meal Cookies, 104, *105*
Almond Milk with Dates, 99
Apple Crostata with Aged Gouda,
40–41, *41*
Apricot Couscous, 112–13
April recipes, 154–55, 157–68, *158*,
161–62, *166*, *169*
Artisan Pizzas, 121, *122–23*
Arugula with Beets and Blood Oranges,
100, 101
August recipes, 239–55, *240*, *243–44*,
246, *250–52*

B

Baby Mac's Organic Granola, *158*, 159
Balsamic Fig Chutney, *28*, 29, *162*, 163
Banyuls wine, 199, 200
barbecue sauce, 222
beef
    filet mignon, *140*, 141
    meatballs, *18*, 19
    New York steak, 16, *17*
    short ribs, *38*, 39
Beet and Carrot Juice, 98
Berries with Spiked Whip, 234, *235*
Bloody Mary Bar, *124*, 126
BLTs with Burrata and Pickled Onions,
252, 254
Blueberry Crumble, *226*, 227
Boucheron cheese, 198, 200
Bouillabaisse with Saffron Aioli
    Crostini, 201–3, *202*
Bourdeaux wine, 199
Braised Short Ribs with Balsamic
    Vinegar, *38*, 39

Buttermilk Mashed Potatoes, 63
Buttermilk Ranch Wedge, *144*, 148,
149
Butternut Squash Soup with Crispy
    Sage, 34, *35*, 59

C

Caesar Salad with Homemade
    Croutons, 120, *120*
Candy Cane Crunch Cookies, 82, 83
Capote, Truman, 85
Carrot Ginger Muffins, 54, *56–57*
Carrot Ginger Soup, 102, *103*
Carrots with Savory Yogurt, 110, *111*
Cauliflower-Reggiano Puree, 20, *20*
Chai Tea Latte, 108, *109*
champagne, 85
    food pairings with, 198, 200
    risotto, *90*, 91
    with vodka-infused berries, *240*, 241
Champagne Lobster Risotto, *90*, 91
Charcuterie 101, *11*, 70–71, 73, 119,
    154–55
    items recommended for, 10
cheese
    bleu, 216–17, 220, 221
    Boucheron, 198, 200
    Brie, 10, 121, *162*, 163
    burger, *144*, 150, 151
    burrata, *244*, 245, *252*, 254
    charcuterie selections of, 10, *11*
    feta, *26*, 27
    goat, 126, *129*, 188, *189*, 198, 200
    Gouda, 10, 40–41, *41*
    Gruyère, 76, *77*, 87, *180*, 182
    La Tur, 10
    Manchego, 10, *232*, 234

    mascarpone, 242, *243*
    with olive tapenade, 188, *189*
    Parmigiano-Reggiano, 19, 20, 64,
        76, *77*, *90*, 91, 248
    Pecorino, 36, 59, *178*, *179–80*
    ricotta, *18*, 19, 73, 178, *179–80*
    St. André, 198
    steak, *130*, 131
    Stilton, 10, 128, *129*, 199, 200
    stuffed in jalapeños, 126, *129*
    wine pairings with, 198–200
chicken
    barbecue, 216–17, 222, *223*
    cheesesteaks, *130*, 131
    roasted, *4–5*, 12
Chicken Cheesesteaks with
    Caramelized Onions and
    Fennel, *130*, 131
Chicken with Jersey Peach BBQ
    Sauce, 216–17, 222, *223*
Child, Julia, 9
chili, 45, *46*
chutney, *28*, 29, *162*, 163
Cipriani restaurants, 175
Classic French Omelette, 9
cocktails
    Bloody Mary Bar, *124*, 126
    Eucalyptus Gin Martini, 75, *75*
    Jalapeño Margarita, *206*, 208
    Rosé Champagne with Vodka-
        Infused Raspberries, *240*,
        241
    Tequila, Lime, Agave, and Club
        Soda, 221
    Vodka Martini with Cerignola
        Olives, 8, *8*
    Whiskey Sour, *147*, 147
    White Peach Bellini, 175

Crab Pots with Lemon Caper Dip, 88, *89*

Crostini with Smashed Pea Puree and Pecorino, 178, *179–80*

Crudités with Arugula Pesto, *176*, 177, *183*

D

Dark Chocolate Fondue
    with Kettle Chips, *72*, 78
    with Strawberries, 119

Decadent Brownies, 153

December recipes, *70–72*, 73–93, *75, 77, 79, 83, 86, 89, 90, 92*

desserts
    Almond Meal Cookies, 104, *105*
    Apple Crostata with Aged Gouda, 40–41, *41*
    Berries with Spiked Whip, 234, *235*
    Blueberry Crumble, *226*, 227
    Candy Cane Crunch Cookies, 82, 83
    Dark Chocolate Fondue with Kettle Chips, *72*, 78
    Dark Chocolate Fondue with Strawberries, 119
    Decadent Brownies, 153
    German Chocolate Cupcakes, 21, *116*, 119
    Good Girl Gone Bad Cookie Shakes, 127, *127*
    Lemon Sgroppino, *192*, 193
    Macadamia Nut Cookies, 83
    Nutella Macaroons, 142
    Port-Poached Pears, *92*, 93
    Pumpkin Pie with Gingersnap Cookie Crust, 68, *69*
    Salted Caramel Plum Tarte Tatin, 204–5, *205*
    Strawberry Mint Cake, 249–51, *250–51*
    Tequila-Marinated Grilled Pineapple, 215

E

Eggplant Towers with Ground Lamb and Yogurt Sauce, 138–39, *139*

eggs
    in omelettes, 9
    in quiche, *180*, 182
    in skillet, 55, 57

Endive Spears with Truffle Honey, 78, *79*

Espresso Affogato, *52*, 55

Eucalyptus Gin Martinis, *75*, 75

F

February recipes, *116*, 119–31, *120, 122–24, 127, 129, 130*

Ficelle Sandwiches with Roasted Turkey, Brie, and Fig Chutney, *162*, 163

Fig, Prosciutto, and Mascarpone Crostini, *242*, *243*

Filet with Au Poivre Sauce, *140*, 141

fish
    bouillabaisse, 201–3, *202*
    crab, 88, *89*, *174*, *180*, 181
    halibut, 230–31, *233*
    lobster, *90*, 91
    mahi mahi, *209*, 212, *213*
    scallops, 168
    shrimp, 26, *27*

Fondue
    with Brussels Sprouts, 87
    with Kettle Chips, *72*, 78
    with Strawberries, 119

French Potato Salad, *216–17*, 224

G

Garten, Ina, 249

German Chocolate Cupcakes, 21, *116*, 119

Goat Cheese-Stuffed Jalapeños, 126, *129*

Goat Cheese with Olive Tapenade, 188, *189*

Good Girl Gone Bad Cookie Shakes, 127, *127*

granola, *158*, 159

gravy, 62–63

Green Bean Casserole with Wild Mushrooms, 66–67

Green Juice with Lemon, 98

Grilled Asparagus and Portobello Mushrooms, *216–17*, 225

Guacamole Salsa, 208, *210*

H

Halibut with Romesco Sauce, 230–31, *233*

Heirloom Tomato and Burrata Bruschetta, *244*, 245

Hemingway Bar, Paris, 241

Herb-Buttered Turkey with Clementine, *60*, 61–63, 65

J

Jalapeño Cheddar Skillet Cornbread with Maple Syrup Drizzle, *46*, 47

Jalapeño Margarita, *206*, 208

January recipes, *94–96*, 97–115, *99, 100, 103, 105–6, 109, 111, 113, 114*

juices, *96*, 97–98

July recipes, *216–17*, 219–34, *220, 223, 226, 232–33, 235*

June recipes, *194–96*, 197–215, *202, 205, 206, 209, 210–11, 213–14*

K

Kale Salad with Pecorino and Truffle Vinaigrette, 36, 59

Keats, John, 211
Kettle Chip and Crème Fraîche–Baked
      Onion Rings, *144, 146–47,* 152

L

Lagered Turkey Chili, 45, *46*
lamb
      chops, *246,* 247
      ground, 138–39, *139*
Lamb Chop Lollipops, *246,* 247
Leek and Asparagus Crustless Quiche,
      180, 182
Lemon Sgroppino, *192, 193*
Lump Crab in Lettuce Cups, *174, 180,*
      181

M

Macadamia Nut Cookies, 83
Mache with Truffle Vinaigrette, 168,
      169
Mahi mahi Tacos with Nectarine Salsa,
      209, 212, 213
March recipes, *132–34, 135–53, 137,*
      139, 140, 144, 146–47, 149–50
May recipes, 173–93, *174, 176, 179–80,*
      183–84, 186, 189, 190–92
Melon Gazpacho, 255
Merlot wine, 198, 200
Monroe, Marilyn, 161
Moroccan Tagine with Preserved
      Lemons, *94,* 112–13, *113*
Mushroom Medley on Olive Crostini,
      166, 167

N

Nectarine Salsa, *210, 212, 213*
New York Steak with Herb Butter,
      16, *17*
November recipes, *50–52,* 53–68,
      56–57, 60, 65, 69
Nutella Macaroons, 142

O

Oak Leaf Lettuces with Balsamic
      Vinaigrette, 44
October recipes, *30–31, 32–49, 34,*
      38, 41, 42, 46

P

pairings, food-wine, 197–99
Pancetta Gougéres, 76, *77*
Pane Vino, Los Angeles, 26
Pat's Steaks, Philadelphia, 131
Pépin, Jacques, 224
Peppermint and Lemon Verbena Tea,
      175
Perriet-Jouët Brut Champagne, 85,
      91, 175
Pete's Tavern, New York City, 1
Pineapple, Cucumber, Coconut Water,
      and Mint juice, 98
pizza, 121, *122–23*
Poblano Chorizo Quesadillas, 209,
      210–11
pork
      bacon, 55, *57, 144, 150, 151, 252,*
            254
      charcuterie selections of, 10, *11*
      chorizo, 209, *210–11*
      pancetta, 188, *189*
      sausage, 64, *65*
Port-Poached Pears, *92, 93*
port wine, *92, 93,* 199, 200
Preserved Lemons, 112–13
Pumpkin Pie with Gingersnap Cookie
      Crust, 68, *69*

Q

quesadillas, 209, *210–11*
quiche, *180,* 182

R

Raoul's, New York City, 141
Ratatouille with Reggiano, *246,* 248
Ricotta Meatballs with Chianti Sauce,
      18, 19
risotto, *90, 91*
Roasted Chicken, *4–5,* 12
Roasted Tomato Linguine, *186, 189–91,*
      190
Romesco Sauce, 230–31, *233*
Rosé Champagne with Vodka-Infused
      Raspberries, *240, 241*
rosé wine, 198, 200, *240, 241*
Rustic Sausage and Fennel Stuffing,
      64, *65*

S

Saffron Aioli, 201
Saint-Émilion, 198, 200
Salad
      Arugula with Beets and Blood
            Oranges, *100, 101*
      Buttermilk Ranch Wedge, *144, 148,*
            149
      Caesar, 120, *120*
      Endive Spears with Truffle Honey,
            78, *79*
      Kale with Pecorino and Truffle
            Vinaigrette, 36, 59
      Lump Crab in Lettuce Cup, *174,*
            180, 181
      Mache with Truffle Vinaigrette,
            168, *169*
      Oak Leaf Lettuces with Balsamic
            Vinaigrette, 44
      with Shallot Vinaigrette, 9
      Slaw with Toasted Pepitas, *210, 214,*
            215
      Spinach with Pancetta, 188, *189*
      Spring Sugar Snap Pea, 160, *161*
      Winter Lettuces with Pomegranate
            Seeds, *86, 87*

Salsa
    Guacamole, 208, *210*
    Nectarine, *210*, 212, *213*
Salted Caramel Plum Tarte Tatin,
    204–5, *205*
Sancerre wine, 198, 200
Sauvignon Blanc wine, 198, 200
Scallops with Jalapeño on Purple Sticky
    Rice, 168
Secret Sauce, 151
September recipes, *4–5, 6–29, 8, 11,*
    14–15, 17–18, 20, 24, 27, 28
Shallot Vinaigrette
    with Simple Salad, 9
    with Spring Sugar Snap Peas, 160,
        161
Shrimp with Feta and Mint, 26, *27*
Sizzling Brown Rice Bowls, 137, *137*
Skillet Eggs with Smoked Bacon and
    Spinach, 55, *57*
Slaw with Toasted Pepitas, *210, 214, 215*
soup
    butternut squash, *34*, 35, 59
    carrot ginger, 102, *103*
    gazpacho, 255
    tlalpeno, *134, 136*
Spiked Hot Chocolate, *42*, 48
Spinach Salad with Pancetta, 188, *189*
Spring Sugar Snap Pea Salad with Fresh
    Mint, 160, *161*
St. André cheese, 198
Stewart, Martha, 21
Stilton
    Dip with Crisp Celery, 128, *129*
    wine pairings with, 199, 200
Strawberry Mint Cake, 249–51, *250–51*
Strawberry-Rhubarb Jam, 28, *28*
Summer Tomatoes with Crumbled Bleu,
    216–17, 220, 221
Super Bowl recipes, *124, 125–31, 127,*
    129–30

T
tacos, *209*, 212, *213*
Tequila, Lime, Agave, and Club Soda,
    221
Tequila-Marinated Grilled Pineapple,
    215
Tlalpeno Soup, *134, 136*
Triple Berry Upside Down Cake, *184,*
    185
Truffle Vinaigrette
    with Kale Salad with Pecorino, 36,
        59
    with Mache, 168, *169*
turkey
    braciola, 13–14, *14–15*
    chili, 45, *46*
    herb-buttered, *60*, 61–63, 65
    sandwiches, *162*, 163
Turkey Braciola, 13–14, *14–15*
Twain, Mark, 49

U
Ultimate Whiskey Bacon Cheeseburger,
    144, 150, 151

V
Vegan Chocolate Truffles, *114*, 115

vinaigrette
    balsamic, 44
    shallot, 9, 160, *161*
    truffle, 36, 59, 168, *169*
Vodka Martini with Cerignola Olives,
    8, *8*
Vongerichten, Jean-Georges, 55

W
Warm Spiced Olives, *106*, 108
whipped cream, 68, *69*
Whiskey Sours, 147, *147*
White Peach Bellinis, 175
wine
    Banyuls, 199, 200
    Bourdeaux, 199
    champagne, 85, *90, 91*, 198, 200,
        240, 241
    Merlot, 198, 200
    pairings with food, 197–200
    port, *92, 93*, 199, 200
    rosé, 198, 200
    Sancerre, 198, 200
    Sauvignon Blanc, 198, 200
Winter Lettuces with Pomegranate
    Seeds, *86*, 87

Z
Zucchini Carpaccio with Manchego,
    232, 234